Chasing Normal

**Finding Love After
Surviving Physical and Emotional Abuse**

LISA GERARDY

Chandler, Arizona

Chasing Normal
Copyright © 2024 by Lisa Gerardy

All rights reserved. This book or any portion thereof may not be reproduced or used in any manner whatsoever without the express written permission of the publisher except for the use of brief quotations in a book review. Direct inquiries to Chasing Normal Media.

Published by Chasing Normal Media
chasingnormalmedia@gmail.com

Names:	Gerardy, Lisa, author.
Title:	Chasing normal : finding love after surviving physical and emotional abuse / Lisa Gerardy.
Description:	Chandler, Arizona : Chasing Normal Media, [2024]
Identifiers:	ISBN: 979-8-9887621-1-9 (Hardcover) | 979-8-9887621-2-6 (Paperback) | 979-8-9887621-3-3 (Ebook) | LCCN: 2024944129
Subjects:	LCSH: Gerardy, Lisa. | Adult child abuse victims—Biography. | Adult child sexual abuse victims--Biography. | Adult children of dysfunctional families—Biography. | Dysfunctional families—Psychological aspects. | Child abuse—Psychological aspects. | Interpersonal relations. | Relationship quality—Psychological aspects. | Mental health. | Self-actualization (Psychology) | Quality of life. | LCGFT: Autobiographies. | BISAC: BIOGRAPHY & AUTOBIOGRAPHY / Memoirs. | FAMILY & RELATIONSHIPS / Dysfunctional Families. | FAMILY & RELATIONSHIPS / Abuse / Child Abuse.
Classification:	LCC: RC569.5.C55 G47 2024 | DDC: 616.85/82239--dc23

Printed in the United States of America

Book Design: Clarity Designworks

979-8-9887621-1-9 (hardcover)
979-8-9887621-2-6 (paperback)
979-8-9887621-3-3 (ebook)

A Note from Lisa

Everything in this memoir is true to the best of my recollection. These are my memories and my perceptions. While others may have different opinions about the events I write about, this is what I experienced and what I remember.

I have tried to tell my story without being too graphic to minimize discomfort. However, if you were abused, there may be triggering moments in the book. I apologize if this happens.

Contents

Introduction: Through the Fog. 1
1973: We don't talk about that 3
1974: Chosen Family. 7
1976: Crayons and Jesus 11
1978: Stomachaches and Bad Grades 17
1979: Halloween in Hollyhood. 21
1979: Roommates 25
1980: Secret Eating and Kiddie City 28
1980: Lesbian Landlady and the Shack of Roaches 32
1980: Orange Trees and Miss Kitty 35
1981: Prime Rib Breakfasts and Rubik's Cube Dreams. 40
1981: Fifth Grade Spy. 43
1982: Yellow on the Fourth of July. 46
1982: Dull Not Shiny 52
1982: Open Psych. 55
1982: Hiding from Rod 64
1982: Merry Fucking Christmas! 67
1983: Tossing Duke 70
1983: Codeine in the Girls' Room 74
1984: The Great Escape 78
1984: Convenience Store Surprise Party 84
1984: Halloween Assholes. 87
1984: As Foretold by Astrology: An Old Man and a Pool 91
1986: Losing my Father for Good 97
1986: The Dad Realization 100

1986: One of these Afternoons 105
1986: The Magic of Alcohol 107
1987: Being Pimped for Weed 109
1988: Ease up, Rambo 113
1988–1989: Will and Me 116
1990: Nice Guy Rebound 123
1991: Group Therapy 127
1993: Coulda Shoulda Been Adopted 130
1993: Young Love 133
1997: Before the Ides of March 139
1996: Comedy Clusterfuck 143
2000: My First Imaginary Mayberry 146
2000: UNCLE Bobby 149
2004: A Maltese and Herpes 151
2005: Dating a REAL Prince 159
2005: Parents, Palm Sunday, and a Period 166
2006: Love and Vomit 169
2006: The Snappiest Place on Earth 171
2007: Moving on Up North 173
2017: Those Fucking Clowns 177
2024: My Man and the Sea 180

Photo Gallery 184
Virtual Hugs 191

Introduction: **Through the Fog**

I can barely see her through the gray mist, even though I am standing right next to her. It's like we are standing in a cloud. It's my mom, Janet, but she is a teen and she's sad. She's wearing a dark dress with a turtleneck, which is weird. I never saw my mom wear a dress in my entire life. She was a pants or jumpsuit person. She wore a pink jumpsuit when she married my stepdad in Vegas. I'm thinking how out of character it is for her to wear a dress, and then I remember how she told me that girls were not allowed to wear pants to school when she was young.

I hug her while she cries, comforting her while thinking of the many times she made me cry when I was little. Janet seems to be feeling guilty about that now, so I choose not to bring any of her episodes up. She tells me that the other kids in high school told her she was too stupid to raise a baby when they found out she was pregnant with my brother. She dropped out of school, married my father, and had one more kid, me, nine years after my brother was born. When my parents separated, she gave my father custody of my brother and kept me.

My chest feels much lighter than it usually does when I am near her, like I had let go of my anger and sadness. I hold her close and tell her that she did what she could. She was young when she became a parent, and her mother was not a good example. My mom told me many stories about how my grandmother made her wear her dead brother's coat to school, stole her lunch money from the kitchen table, and scrubbed her teeth with Comet cleaning powder.

I continue comforting my teen mother while she shakes and wipes her tears with her hand. I can't help but remember that time when I was seven I wiped my tears with my hand after forgetting I had just spread Bengay menthol cream on my mother's back and shoulders. I must not have done a good enough job of it because she got very angry at me. I wasn't massaging hard enough. I tried my best, but my hands hurt. My best wasn't good enough that day. A short time after this, she purchased "Burt the Bunny," a wooden rolling massager shaped like a rabbit. This made it more fun to massage my mother's back.

Even though I am hugging her, I can barely see her blonde curls through the fog. She seems even shorter than her adult height of four foot eleven, and she's thin. Janet was always thick from head to toe, like I am now. "You fed me," I tell her. "You loved me in your own way," I add, trying to console her. I almost say, "And you never threw me across the room," but then I remember that she told me she had done that when I was a baby. I landed on the couch and was okay, according to her. I'm not sure why she even told me. I'm not sure that I have ever been totally okay.

Even with that flying baby vision in my head, I keep hugging her. I tell her she did what she could at the time and she snapped sometimes. I tell her all mothers snap, and that I snapped with my son, Richie, too. I never threw him, though. I think that throwing a baby is a bit beyond snapping, but I hold that in and tell her I forgive her.

I feel a firm pat on my arm, and then a hand grabs that arm and shakes me. It's my husband waking me. Apparently, the alarm went off. I'm still in a fog when I sit up; this one is only mental. It's not my first Janet dream since her death, but it's the first time I forgave her.

1973 | We don't talk about that

While some people's first memories are presents around a Christmas tree or blowing out candles on a birthday cake, my first memory could have easily landed my family on Dr. Phil. We were so screwed up that I think even a reality TV doctor could have done wonders for us.

When I was two, my mom decided to leave her second husband, Ronnie, after only a few months of marriage. My mom loved to tell the story of me at their wedding, wearing a white dress and shiny white Mary-Janes, proudly carrying a purse. Apparently, when the minister asked if anyone had a reason why my mom and Ronnie should not be married, I held up my purse and said, "I got my puss!" I still call my purse a "puss" to this day. And I was right about their wedding. It shouldn't have happened.

Ronnie didn't agree with this whole divorce thing and wouldn't let go. According to Mom, he "had a gun and was not a nice guy." Ronnie scared her enough to make her move back to Peoria, Illinois, from Hollywood, Florida. Mom had moved away from the Midwest about eight years earlier when my father, Gary, got a news producer job at Channel 10 in Miami for Sally Jessy Raphael's show. After my parents divorced, my mom decided to stay and do the single mom thing in South Florida. She figured it would be easier without snow to shovel. Then, she decided to remarry.

So, in the car we went, with as many belongings as the car could hold and still allow space for an infant to lie in the back seat. My brother, Tony, was left in Florida with our father. He was nine years older than me, and my mom just didn't want to bring him. Before this move to Peoria, she was already in the process of giving up custody of Tony. My brother wanted to try living with our father for a bit because he would have a dog and his own room — instead of his green sleeping bag in our living room. My father wasn't sending child support to my mom, so we lived in a tiny one-bedroom apartment with a window air conditioner unit. My mom told Tony that if he wanted to live with our father, she would take him to court and make it legal. As promised, my mom, my father, and my twelve-year-old brother went to court. The judge asked my brother if he wanted to live with our father, and he said, "Yes." A few months later, Tony figured out that life with my father was not any better. My father would beat my brother for anything. He once felt the bar of soap after Tony took a shower and beat him because the soap wasn't wet enough. When Tony asked my mom if he could live with us again, she said no. Years later, when I was ten, Mom explained it this way, "He chose his father so fuck him." She also referred to him as my "mangy brother" and insisted that my father didn't make him wash his face or brush his teeth.

Like I said, we were prime candidates for Dr. Phil.

Mom and I made the drive up to Peoria and moved in with my grandmother, her second husband, Pat, and his son, Norman. Norman was about fourteen at this time and seemed nice. I was only two, but I remember he paid a lot of attention to me, and I loved this, of course. What little kid doesn't like attention?

We didn't live in my grandmother's house very long before the weird shit started. I had already been living in a single-parent home and not having a relationship with my father to screw me up, but at age two, the granddaddy of all issues came into play – Norman began sexually abusing me.

My mother was working at a hospital in Peoria, so my grandmother was supposed to watch me. Sometimes, Grandma would need, or rather want, to go out, so she would have Norman babysit me. Since I was young, most of my memories are hazy. Unfortunately, the only vivid memories I have are the ones centered around abuse.

The first memory of the abuse is sort of innocent. It was night, and I was home alone with Norman. We were both lying on our sides on the couch in the front room of my grandmother's house. Norman was lying behind me on the scratchy plaid couch with his arms around me, spooning me. I remember it felt good to be hugged, even though he seemed to be hugging me too tightly, and his hands sometimes went to weird places on my body. As I still considered Norman to be nice, I did what he told me to do. Then, I remember seeing headlights reflecting on the wall from the front window, and Norman told me to pretend that I was asleep. I guess he wanted it to look like he had gotten me to sleep by comforting me. I closed my eyes and pretended to sleep.

The next thing I remember is the first time Norman forced me to perform oral sex on him. Again, I was two. TWO. I was sitting on his lap in the recliner just outside of Grandma's bedroom. The house was small, and my grandmother's room was directly off the living room. I don't think anyone was home. It was dark. The big old floor model TV was on, tuned in to a 1970s cop show. The noise of the TV and the flickering lights are still in my memory. At some point, Norman showed me his "alive." That is what he called it because it moved on its own. He told me to give it a kiss. Since I was always blowing kisses at everyone, I gave it a little peck. Norman wanted more than that and got angry when I started crying. He pushed me off of his lap, and I landed right in front of "Baretta" while hearing "Keep Your Eye on the Sparrow," feeling acid rise in my throat.

After that, I was alone in the kitchen with my grandmother. While we were standing in front of the refrigerator, I tried to tell her about what was happening with Norman. Her eyes turned cold and blank, and she told me never to talk about that again. I shut up immediately and never said another word about it to her.

Later, when I was alone in the kitchen, feeling embarrassed and sad, I opened the refrigerator and stuck my finger in the baking soda box, licking the powder from my fingers. It tasted horrible, and while I never ate baking soda again, I ate a lot of other things over the years in an attempt to deal with the feelings that I didn't understand and wasn't allowed to talk about. I learned to hold things in that day. I got the message that no one would help me anyway.

We moved back to Florida not too long after this. I was glad to get out of my grandmother's house. I didn't feel warm and protected there like kids are supposed to feel at their grandparents' houses. My mom was glad to get out, too. I'm not sure if my mother was sicker of Peoria itself or her mother. As my mother told it, she had no money, no job, and no place to live in Florida, but she still left Peoria before the weather started to get too cold that year. Either way, we went back to the land of palm trees and tourists. I know that sounds like heaven, but it soon turned into hell.

1974 | Chosen Family

I sat there on the cement porch step with Delbert and sipped a small teacup of prune juice, clutching the handle tightly so I wouldn't drop it and break the cup. I was afraid to break the cup because I didn't want Ilene or Delbert to hit me like my mom did when I broke something at home. I had begged to try some when I saw Delbert and Ilene drinking tiny glasses of prune juice with their toast at their yellow Formica kitchen table when my mom dropped me off on the way to work. My mom took a receptionist job at Children's Medical Center, even though she had wanted her old insurance clerk job, which had been filled. And that is why I was sitting on the step with Delbert, drinking prune juice, not knowing I would be sitting on the toilet soon after.

An hour or so after drinking the prune juice, I was sitting on Ilene and Delbert's toilet with my feet hanging above the floor. I was holding a yellow-knitted doll that hid an extra roll of toilet paper to my stomach, trying to push the cramps away. The Florida sun came through the privacy window above the tub and made me sweat. I hated stomachaches, but I got them often. When I was finally done, Ilene came in and cleaned me up. I thought about how she would make a good grandma.

Mom and I met Delbert and Ilene when we arrived back in Florida a few months earlier. Lucky for us, my mom had kept in touch with her best friend, Angie, from her insurance clerk job. So, at least we had a place to stay. While we were staying with her, my mom searched the newspaper for jobs, and the part-time housekeeping job for Delbert and Ilene, an old couple in Hallandale, was the first thing she found. It worked out well because she could bring me with her. There was no one at Angie's to watch me during the day and my father, Gary, had no interest in spending any time with me.

Gary didn't even think I was really his child, or at least that is what he told the judge. There wasn't DNA testing then, so his reasoning was that I had "oriental eyes." Once Gary got custody of Tony, he told my mom that he didn't have to pay her child support for me since they each had one kid, and I wasn't his anyway. The judge disagreed, and my dad sent an occasional check with Tony when he visited. It wasn't enough.

Laura, Pete, and their newly divorced daughter Fran lived next door to Delbert and Ilene. Sometimes, in the afternoon, Laura and Pete liked to sit out on the porch, drinking cans of beer and smoking cigarettes. Fran was usually at work at the front desk of the Singapore Hotel in Miami when this was going on. Laura was nice and waved at me and winked when I stared at her shoulder-length gray hair. I wasn't used to seeing old ladies with longer hair. I quickly hid behind Ilene when Laura caught me staring at her. My shyness didn't last long. I started spending more time on the porch next door and got to know and love Laura. Laura felt the same and offered to watch me when Delbert and Ilene could not. I wished Laura could be my grandma, along with Ilene. They were both so much nicer than my real grandma.

Not long after we met them, Laura, Pete, and Fran moved to Hollywood, to a triplex on Taylor Street. At this time, my mom and I were living in a tiny efficiency and Mom was looking for a bigger place, at least a one-bedroom apartment. When Laura told us that the back unit of the triplex was available, we moved, too. I was so happy to be near Laura and Fran.

After we moved to Taylor Street, Laura became my babysitter. She was kind and gave me lots of cigarette-scented hugs. Her husband, Pete, was scary in my mind. He was a World War Two veteran with limited mobility, and he would sit in a wheelchair and yell at The Young and the Restless. He hated Victor, the villain on the show. His yelling and rough voice scared me. I tried to stay away from Pete as much as possible.

The year before I started Kindergarten, Fran took over as my primary babysitter. Laura was getting older and was sick. I didn't know what cancer was, and I didn't understand how sick Laura was until she died when I was in first grade. By this time, Fran had stopped working at the hotel and stayed home with her parents to help them. She also helped me by introducing me to Sesame Street and books. I learned all my letters and numbers with Fran. I also learned about gardening and loving animals, especially cats. Fran had a bunch of cats inside and outside.

Fran was the same age as my mom, 32, but she seemed so much younger. Fran was fun and nice. She took me everywhere with her in her old, gray car without air conditioning. It was hot, but we cranked the windows down and let the breeze in. I was always in the front seat with Fran. Even though the car was old, the radio worked fine. I would sing along with Fran and Elton John, really popping my lips on the B sounds for "Benny and the Jets." I grew to love Fran, maybe more than I loved my mom.

At night, when her parents went to bed, and I was at home with my mom, Fran partied. She would go dancing and drinking with her friends. Sometimes, when I arrived in the morning, she would look like she didn't feel good. She'd put me in front of the TV to watch Sesame Street while she drank a cup of tea and relaxed with a cold rag on her head. I was a quiet kid, anyway, but I was told to "just play quietly" when Fran had a headache.

One morning in 1978, after Fran had been caring for me for a few years, she was in the bathroom vomiting when I arrived on her porch. Pete told me to come in through the screen door, so I reached up, pushed the door handle, and walked in. I turned around and waved to my mom, who was waiting by her old, green car to make sure I made it to Fran's okay. I had the day off from first grade, and I was spending the whole day with Fran instead of just going home with her after school. Pete had the morning news on the TV, and he pointed to the couch without really looking at me. I sat on the vinyl couch and pet a gray cat who had jumped up when I sat down.

When Fran came out of the bathroom, she did not look good. She said, "Hi" to me and walked into the kitchen to make herself some burnt toast. Fran told me that burnt toast was the only thing that helped her stop throwing up. Fran offered me some, and I shook my head no and made a face. I felt like I would vomit if I ate charred bread.

A few weeks after that day, when Fran picked me up from school, she told me the most exciting news ever. She was going to have a baby. I was so happy because I thought this baby would be like a brother or sister to me. Nicole was born a week before my seventh birthday. Mom and I went to Hollywood Memorial to see Fran and Nicole. Fran walked with us to the nursery to look at Nicole through the window. Fran pointed to Nicole and said, "Look at her bald head."

I took offense to this and frowned at Fran and said, "She's NOT bald." I loved Nicole at first sight, and I felt like a big sister.

1976 | Crayons and Jesus

There I was, four years old, in the back of my mom's rust bucket of a green Chevy in Hollywood, Florida. Mom was driving, and Fran sat in the front seat while we made our way from our side-by-side duplexes on Taylor Street to St. Mark's Lutheran School on Filmore and 28th Avenue. Even though we were on Section 8 and Food Stamps, Mom did not want me to go to public school. I was nervous about going to any school, even though I knew I would finally learn to do this magical reading stuff that the grown-ups could do, and I knew I could eventually become a "reshistered nurse." My mom had worked in doctors' offices my whole life, and I had come to love the kind nurses who picked me up and kissed my cheeks when Mom brought me in for a visit.

I had a bad stomachache that morning while I was putting on my white Mary Janes. I had just learned how to buckle my own shoes, so I wanted to wear these shoes all the time. I told my mom I was nervous about going to school and that I didn't want to go. She told me I should be excited about school because I could wear pants if I wanted. She told me how she had to wear dresses or skirts to school when she was little. Girls weren't allowed to wear pants. I thought this was odd, but it didn't take my nervousness away. I didn't love pants all that much.

When it was time to go to school, Fran walked over to our duplex, and we all rode to St. Mark's together in that ugly green car. I slid back and forth on the vinyl back seat while my mom made the short drive to the school. When we pulled into the parking lot, the butterflies in my stomach kicked into high gear. Groaning, my stomach started cramping, and I said, "Oh no!" Knowing that fear was the sole source of my stomachache, Fran laughed and told me I was going to be fine. She reminded me that I already knew the alphabet and my numbers because she had taught them to me. Fran also reminded me that I would learn to read because she knew I really loved books.

My mom parked the car, and we all walked to Mrs. Stark's kindergarten class. I had thought her name was Mrs. Star, which would have been cool until the adults explained it was Stark, not Star. After saying hello to me, my mom, and Fran, Mrs. Stark showed me where my seat was and told me I could go play in the playroom with the other kids until class started. I waved bye to my mom and Fran and skipped into the play area. I had recently discovered skipping, and it was my chosen method of transportation.

The playroom was a smaller room within the classroom, sort of like an office cubical. There was a play kitchen set, Legos, books, some dolls, and other toys. There were other kids in there, being kind of loud. I was used to hanging out with grown-ups who were much quieter. I already wanted to leave.

Then, Mrs. Stark called all the students out of the playroom so she could start class. I ignored her. I stayed in the playroom and looked at everyone through the small opening between the cubical walls. Mrs. Stark noticed me there but didn't force me to come out. She told the kids that they were going to sing "This Little Light," and everyone but me knew what she was talking about. That's because the other kids also went to St. Mark's church. I was the only one who was new to St. Mark's. Feeling like a misfit, I stayed in the playroom while the rest of the kids sang about Jesus being a light or something. I eventually came out of the playroom and learned that song, along with the accompanying blowing of the finger, to signify someone trying to blow out that little light.

I grew to like St. Mark's a lot. All the kids were nice, and we had a great playground. This is where I learned to fear the teeter-totter. It seemed like a good idea when I jumped on it one day with a girl from my class until she sat all the way down on it, and I was way up high. I had always hated heights right from the beginning. I wasn't that high up, but it felt scary, and I screamed to be brought back down where I could get off this torture contraption.

I became more comfortable with Mrs. Stark and the kids the longer I went to St. Mark's. I was still a little shy, though. One day, Mrs. Stark decided to test us on the alphabet. She did this by holding up laminated cards with letters on them and asking us what they were. I will never forget when she held up a capital F and asked me what letter it was. I was so embarrassed. It felt like all the kids were just staring at me. I didn't want to speak in front of the class so I claimed not to know what that letter was. I'm not sure why I thought that was a better option than just saying "F." Mrs. Stark sent a note home with me after school that she pinned on my shirt so Fran would see it as soon as she picked me up. Fran watched me after school until my mom got home. She was PISSED at Mrs. Stark after she read the note. It said something to the effect of "Lisa does not know her ABCs." Fran knew I knew them because she had taught them to me.

The next day, when she picked me up from school, Fran came into my classroom to talk to Mrs. Stark. After a couple of minutes, they called me over to Mrs. Stark's desk. Mrs. Stark held up the F again and asked me what letter it was. I said, "F." Then she held up other letters and asked me what they were. I got them all correct.

"Lisa, why didn't you just respond when I held up the F yesterday?"

Shoulders slumped, I pretended to study the terrazzo floor underneath my feet. "I don't know."

But I did know. I just didn't want to tell her the truth that my mind had gone blank because I'd been scared. How was I supposed to think when everyone was looking at me?

I always felt a little different at St. Mark's because I didn't go to church on Sunday with everyone. I also didn't buy into this whole God and Jesus thing. However, I still really wanted to be Mary in the Christmas play because that was the best role. Instead, I was just one of the angels in the chorus. Darlene played Mary, and the boy I had a crush on, Vance, got the part of Joseph. I was jealous.

The budget for costumes was pretty low, so St. Mark's ordered our graduation gowns early and tasked the parents with sewing silver garland around the arms of the gowns. Since my mom didn't sew and worked full time, Fran made my angel costume and halo. Even though I was still mad about not being Mary, I have to admit…I loved my angel dress.

I continued going to St. Mark's until the first half of first grade. Compared to kindergarten, first grade at St. Mark's was challenging for me because we had to start memorizing Bible verses every week. Since we didn't go to church, I didn't have a big interest in Christianity. Sure, I'd heard the Jesus stories in school, and I knew people thought the Bible was some magical book from God, but I had no interest in learning what that book had to say. Plus, the school was using the King James version, and the thees, thous, and thines did not exactly roll off of my six-year-old tongue. I remember waiting until the last minute to memorize my verse every morning. I would sit at the kitchen table, eating my oatmeal or cereal, and try to commit a Bible verse to memory.

Halfway through first grade, two important things happened. The positive thing was Fran would bring my "cousin" Nicole into my life. The negative thing was that my mom realized that private school was way out of her single-mom budget, so she took me out of St. Mark's and enrolled me in Colbert Elementary School.

I was surprised Mom put me in Colbert because it was more diverse than St. Marks, and Mom wasn't the biggest fan of Black people. She made that clear whenever we were driving around town.

"Lock your doors! We're going through Black Town!" my mom yelled back to me from behind the wheel as she drove her huge, green Chevy jalopy down 24th Avenue towards Washington Street in Hollywood, Florida. To her, that intersection was some sort of border into fear.

My big brother was visiting us that weekend and he was sitting up front with Mom. When Mom yelled to lock the doors, I got scared instantly. "Why do we have to lock the doors? What are they going to do?" I asked from the back seat.

"Just do it, Seece!" my older brother yelled from the front passenger seat, using his nickname for me. I called myself "Sisa Ne" instead of "Lisa Rene" when I was little. My brother just couldn't let it die. He called me "Sisa" for the rest of his life.

As if our lives depended on it, I slid across the hot, green vinyl back seat, scratching my legs on the rips in the material as I punched the locks on both of the car's back doors. No one wore seatbelts in 1977, so I could slide back and forth pretty easily, except for my legs sticking to the seat as I moved. Once I had the doors locked, I sat in the middle of the seat, away from the windows. I wasn't sure why my mom was so worried about driving through "Black Town," but her tone alone was enough to terrify me. It made me think that the people who lived there would attack us.

Soon after this frantic door-locking episode, I started going to Colbert Elementary. I wasn't supposed to go to Colbert. Oakridge, a much better public school, was our neighborhood school. Mom lied about our address and put me in Colbert because her friend Sally's kids went there, and I could get a ride home with her and go to her house after school when Fran couldn't come and get me. Going from a private school to a public elementary school was stressful, no matter which school it was.

A day or two after changing schools, it was discovered that I had lice. Fran picked me up from school early and made me sit on the porch so she could start picking the nits from my hair. Mom stopped at Eckerd on her way home and got lice shampoo. That evening was spent with bug-killing foam on my head and my sheets soaking in a bathtub filled with bleach and water. We didn't have a washing machine.

The next morning, Mom called the school to talk about this whole lice thing. She was pissed at the school because she assumed that was where I caught them. She told the office lady, "My daughter caught lice from all of the n------ there!" It was 1978, and the n-word was still said pretty regularly. The office receptionist very calmly explained to Mom that lice prefer Caucasian hair because we do not put oil in it.

Mom slammed the phone down so hard that it made a ringing sound. I could tell she wanted me to go back to St. Marks, but that was not an option. Colbert was free, and Mom was broke. Having no money was one of the reasons she started dating an abusive alcoholic named Rod.

1978 | **Stomachaches and Bad Grades**

We heard my mom's car pull into her parking spot from Fran's bedroom window, where we were lying in bed reading and Nicole was in the crib chewing on a rattle. The windows were open because Fran never used the air conditioning during the day. It made the electric bill too high. I turned and looked through the screen at my mom's green car in the parking space next door. My stomach started to hurt because I had gotten my report card for the third quarter that day, and it wasn't good. It was my first bad report card.

"She's home," I said to Fran while putting a bookmark in the Bobbsey Twins book Fran had given me to read. Fran put her book down and said, "Well, let's go over there." Fran knew I was nervous. Fran picked up Nicole and carried her on her right hip, holding my hand with her left.

I saw the look on Fran's face when she handed my report card to my mom as we walked into the duplex. My mom was putting her purse down and kicking off her shoes next to the black-and-white couch. Fran had already looked at my report card and knew my mom would explode when she saw the low grades and the comments about me not doing work. And explode she did as soon as Fran and Nicole went home.

"LISA RENE PETTY!" she yelled even though I was standing about three feet from her. I looked down at the red carpet and started to get tears in my eyes. I was only seven, but I had already experienced what happened when I disappointed my mom. She shoved the report card in my face and yelled, "You better start doing your work, or I will beat your ass!" She smacked the report card down on the top of my head.

Mom wasn't bluffing. She had beaten my ass many times already. She also threw dishes, glasses, knick-knacks, anything breakable, and slammed doors like it was an Olympic event. The tears were running down my face, and my nose was stuffy. "I will, Mommy," I said, promising to do my work while covering my face with my hands.

"You better! Now, go wash your face. Rod is coming to take us out to dinner." I thought she had stopped seeing him after he left bruises on her arms. Rod was a security guard my mom had met at the bank when I was in first grade. They had been dating for over a year at this point. He was married and an abusive alcoholic. My stomach started to hurt, and I felt sick. My mom was mad at me, AND Rod was coming over.

When my mom first started dating him, Rod seemed like a good guy. He bought me a beautiful blue faux fur coat. When you are six years old, poor, and living in South Florida, fake fur is rather interesting. I have pictures somewhere of me wearing that coat with a big smile on my face, standing in front of a palm tree. Any time it got below seventy, I wanted to wear my fur. Of course, this happened maybe twice the entire time I fit into the coat.

Rod also took us out to eat a lot, which we loved. I remember going to a great breakfast spot in Hallandale and ordering way too much food. My mom tried to get me to order a small kid's breakfast, but I didn't want that. Rod let me order what I wanted.

Rod took us to a Chinese restaurant on US1 pretty regularly and introduced me to egg drop soup, which is still my favorite. I can remember my mom getting mad when he ordered a drink, but I was so enamored with my Shirley Temple that I didn't care. As I got to know Rod, and as I listened in on his arguments with my mom, I learned it would be better not to have a fur coat and Shirley Temples than be around this monster.

For starters, Rod was married, and this made my mom angry, even though she knew that from the beginning. It didn't make her angry enough to leave the relationship, though. Rod also had a hell of a drinking problem. He was a mean drunk. When he had too much, he would hit my mom.

And here my mom was telling me that he was on his way over to our apartment to take us out right after she yelled at me for my bad report card. I wished I had listened to my friends at school so my mom wouldn't be mad. Jenny and Audra had tried to help me.

I had stopped doing my work at school earlier that spring. "Just copy our work!" Jenny stage whispered at me while pushing her purple math ditto towards me. Audra sat next to her and nodded quietly while looking at Miss Johnson, our teacher, who sat at her desk grading spelling tests. She let us work in groups of three to complete our subtraction worksheet. Colbert had a lot more students than St. Marks, so teachers were probably a little overwhelmed. I didn't feel like working, so I just sat there and stared at the numbers on the sheet until they blurred.

"Lisa, come up here, please," Miss Johnson said. Jenny and Audra gave me a look that said, "You should have just copied our work."

I turned my body to the left to exit my one-piece desk, cubby, and seat. I was wearing shorts, and my chubby thighs made an embarrassing gassy noise against the wooden seat. Jenny and Audra looked down at their papers, and a couple of boys laughed at me. I walked up to Miss Johnson's desk and looked down at my dirty white sneakers.

"Lisa, you haven't been doing your work. Why not?" Miss Johnson was a nice teacher, and I hated disappointing her, but my stomach hurt all the time, and I just couldn't force myself to concentrate on dittos, workbooks, and stories. All I thought about was Rod hurting my mom and my mom hurting me.

I looked at Miss Johnson's concerned face and shrugged my reply. I looked back down.

Miss Johnson wasn't giving up. She asked the question that teachers usually ask: "Is anything going on at home?"

I thought about telling her everything about my mom hitting me and screaming over any little thing. About Rod coming over drunk and hurting my mom. About having stomach aches every day because I never knew when someone would be scary angry. But I couldn't tell her because I knew if I did, my mom would lie and say everything was fine, and then she would punish me for telling on her. I replied, "No. Everything is fine."

Everything was not fine. I had recently witnessed Rod abuse my mom. My mom screamed, and I came running out of my room, where I was reading with my stuffed animals, and sped down the short red-carpeted hallway.

My mom and Rod were in the kitchen. She was crying, "YOU'RE HURTING ME!" Rod had her pressed against the counter and did not see me walk in. I was scared but also angry. My mom wasn't perfect, but she was MY mom. She was the only parent I had. Without thinking too long, I opened the drawer where the two steak knives were and grabbed one.

"STOP HURTING MY MOM!" I yelled at Rod, holding up a steak knife. He turned around and laughed. He told me to put the knife down before I hurt myself. I continued to stand there, gripping the knife until he stepped away from my mom.

"GET OUT!" my mom yelled. I put the knife back in the drawer and stood with my back against the drawer, figuring I would keep Rod from getting my weapon. Rod smirked and took his keys out of the pocket of his brown security guard uniform pants. He walked out the door and slammed it on the way out. I wish I could say we never saw him again, but Mom and Rod's "relationship" would last for seven years.

1979 | Halloween in Hollyhood

I spun around in my homemade Wonder Woman Costume and waved my gold spray-painted lasso. Mom and Fran took pictures of me and the flashes hurt my eyes. Nicole sat in her stroller in a clown costume. Fran had made both of our costumes.

Fran had been making my costumes since I was four and went trick-or-treating as Cinderella, but the Wonder Woman costume was my favorite one. In the mid to late seventies, Linda Carter played Wonder Woman on a prime-time show. This was way before DVRs and streaming, but I'm pretty sure I never missed an episode. Every week, I ran barefoot across the rough red carpet in the duplex on Taylor Street, from the bathroom to the TV. My mom made me take my nightly bath before I could watch TV.

I couldn't miss an episode. I wanted to be a brave hero like Wonder Woman. I talked about her all the time. Listening to me ramble on about invisible planes and tiaras and lassos inspired Fran to make this awesome costume. She even loaned me a dark wig. I was in heaven. I was certain I WAS Wonder Woman until some old lady ruined it for me.

There were a couple of small apartment buildings in my neighborhood. We lived in a duplex, and Fran and Nicole lived in the triplex next door, but there was also a "big" three-story building right next door to our duplex, on the other side of the long thorny hedge. Most of the tenants in these buildings were elderly. Florida is "God's waiting room," after all. When we went trick-or-treating, we stayed close to our duplex. We covered about half of our block, so going to that apartment building was essential.

Most of the time, the older people were very nice. They had candy ready. If they didn't have candy, they would drop pennies or nickels in my bag, which I could exchange for gumballs when we went shopping at Pantry Pride. I was excited about getting cash or candy.

Some of the older people were grouchy. They would sit in their living rooms with the curtains open and ignore us. One man sat there with the TV blaring, looked right at us, and didn't come to the door. I walked to the next door. After all, there appeared to be hundreds of apartments, but my mom told me to wait a minute. She stood there and yelled a string of obscenities at the man. I'm not sure what she thought this would accomplish. He remained in his seat.

A couple of doors after this, a nice older lady answered the door. I said, "Trick-or-treat" and held out my bag. She backed away a little and asked to see my costume. I moved my bag off to the side and did a spin for her. She looked me up and down and smiled. She turned her head to the woman sitting in the living room and said, "Grace! Look at this! It's Miss America!"

I was crushed. Clearly, I was Wonder Woman. Was this old lady blind? Fran and my mom tried to explain to her that I was Wonder Woman but after several rounds of "You know, Wonder Woman. The superhero" and "Who?" they gave up. Mom said, "Fuck it. You're Miss America." I shrugged and walked to the next apartment with my heavy candy bag.

A couple of years later, my mom and Fran got into a big fight. I think it started because Fran told my mom she thought she was too hard on me. My mom was always a screaming, yelling, hitting kind of mom, and since Fran was our neighbor during a big chunk of my childhood, she could hear the abuse, and she could see how timid I was around my mom. Fran was the opposite. She didn't yell or get angry, really. She was very calm and soothing. Like a lot of parents, my mom didn't take kindly to being told how to parent. So, she got really angry at Fran and told her to screw off. She didn't talk to Fran for at least a year, and after that argument, I wasn't allowed to accept Halloween costumes from her anymore.

For the rest of my trick-or-treating days, I wore those horrible plastic costumes from the store. People who grew up in the 70s and 80s know what I'm talking about. Back when parents didn't care about our health as much, they let us wear hard plastic masks with tiny breathing holes. The costume portion was nothing but a colored trash bag. The entire ensemble could be marketed as a weight loss suit and a Halloween costume. In Florida, you sweat in October anyway; wearing a trash bag could be deadly. Our parents did not even send us out with water bottles. If these costumes existed today, the owner of the company would get a thorough thrashing from the *Today Show*, and every mommy blogger on the planet would launch a "Let our children breathe" campaign.

Not only were the costumes uncomfortable, but they were also just all-around shitty looking. I remember one year, I had some sort of Spider-Woman costume. I'm not talking about Spiderman's lady friend. I mean, it was a garish yellow costume, and the mask had some sort of spidery crown on it. I still don't know what the heck I was trying to be that year.

A year after we moved from the Taylor Street to the Wilson Street chopped-up house, my mom took me trick-or-treating. We still weren't seeing Fran and Nicole at this time, and it was just Mom and me walking around the neighborhood. This neighborhood didn't have as many apartments, so I remember getting less candy. One guy opened the door like we'd interrupted something law enforcement should have been alerted to. He seemed creepy, like the kind of guy who probably had children buried under his house.

Mom and I tried to leave once we saw him standing there, as he seemed totally unprepared for Halloween. He insisted that we wait, and he went back into his house. He came back with an apple and put it in my bag. Mom and I said thank you and got the hell away from that door. When we got home and started going through the candy, we noticed that the apple had some puncture marks and cat fur on it. We were going to throw it away anyway because everyone believed people put razor blades in apples in the 80s. The cat fur solidified our decision. I have always loved cats, but even at ten, I wasn't going to eat their fur.

At this time, Fran, Nicole, and Fran's father, Pete, lived in the cottage behind the cut-up Wilson Street house, so we slowly started to see Fran and Nicole again. My mom and Fran never apologized to each other, not that Fran had any reason to apologize, and their relationship would never be as close. My mom held a grudge against Fran for the rest of her life. Mom was jealous because she could see that I felt safer with Fran. Somehow, she couldn't figure out how to make me feel safe with her.

1979 : **Roommates**

In the fall, when I had started third grade, Norman, the abusive step-uncle, came to live with my mother and me in Florida. From what I could overhear when my mother talked to my grandmother on the phone, Norman was having trouble in school and was too much for grandmother and grandfather to handle. So, the adults thought it would be a good idea for Norman to live with my mom and me, her eight-year-old daughter, in Florida in our two-bedroom apartment.

I remember this apartment well. Aside from all the bad things that happened in it, this was one of my favorite apartments. This was the place with the red carpeting and a black-and-white sofa. Black and red are still my favorite colors. There was also a golden-colored chaise lounge in the living room corner across from the TV. Sometimes, during the summer or if I were home sick on a school day, I would spend almost the whole day in that chaise. I would even eat there while watching cartoons.

The only furniture that did not come with the apartment was the small brown bar and bar stools that my mom had purchased. My mom was never a drinker, so it was an odd purchase for a single mom. She kept the bar well-stocked, or at least it looked that way when I was eight and sat on the carpet behind it tasting the Galliano lid.

The apartment's master bedroom was an efficiency, with its own entrance. It did not have a kitchen, just a bedroom and a bathroom. The entrance led to the driveway of the triplex next door.

"Aunt" Fran, her daughter Nicole, and Fran's dad lived there. That's another reason that I loved that apartment. I loved being near Fran.

At one point, my mom couldn't afford to rent the apartment as a two-bedroom apartment, so the landlady locked the deadbolt on the master bedroom door and rented the efficiency to someone else. Mom and I would share a bedroom then. The funny thing was that an air vent opened from our hallway into the efficiency's closet. So, we had no privacy, and neither did the other tenant. I could hear everything that went on over there. I always wondered if they knew I was home alone or if they heard me crying.

When Norman came to live with us, we still had both bedrooms. Mom had the master bedroom, and Norman shared a room with me. Yes, you read that right. A teenage boy, sixteen by this time, was supposed to share a room with a little girl. Even though Mom didn't know what had happened back in Peoria since my grandmother told me never to talk about it, this was still a bad idea.

Norman slept in a twin bed in my room, and I slept in the other twin bed. Previously, Norman's bed had been home to my stuffed animals. They had to be moved to a garbage bag in the closet to make room for him, which I wasn't happy about because I thought they would suffocate.

Norman was acting normally for a while. Then, one day, Mom had to bring me home early from school for vomiting on the playground. When Norman got home from high school, Mom went back to work, leaving him to care for me. I got nervous, but I said nothing.

I was lying on the black-and-white couch eating potato chips when Norman decided he wanted to "play a game." He unzipped his pants, and I felt sick. He forced my head down. I'm sure he must have said something first, trying to persuade me that this was a good idea, but I don't remember any of that. I just remember vomiting potato chips all over the sofa. He smacked me, and I started crying from the vomiting and from being smacked. Neither one of us mentioned any of this to my mom when she got home. I was afraid she would be mad at me for vomiting on the couch.

Later, it could have been days, months, or weeks, Norman abused me for the last time. It was night, a school night, and I had a bad dream and woke Norman with my crying. He told me to come over to his bed. I'm not sure why I complied, but I got into his bed. At first, he held me and comforted me, and I started dozing. The next thing I remember, Norman was on top of me with his pants off. He pulled down my pajama pants and told me, "It's okay. You'll make it. It's okay." I didn't think it was okay. I don't know where I got the energy, but I got out from under him and ran into my mother's room, where she was sleeping with Rod.

I climbed into bed beside my mom and, through sobs, told her what happened. Rod, who was a scary person to me, went into full-on hero mode. He got out of bed and went into my room to get Norman. I hid under my mom's covers. I heard yelling and something slamming against the wall. Norman was told to sleep on the couch, and I was sent back to my room to try to sleep for the rest of the night. The next day, I was sent to school. I never saw a doctor, nor was I taken to any sort of therapist. That was that. Life went on. It was like nothing had happened.

After school, Norman was sent home on a plane. Before he left, he was sitting at the little bar in our apartment with my brother, Tony. Norman and Tony were close in age and always got along well. They were talking about how horrible it was that Norman had to leave. I was relieved and couldn't wait for him to leave. Tony was angry at me and blamed me for this. He asked me why I "lied" about this. I was stunned. I couldn't believe my big brother was not taking my side. That's the day that I decided I didn't like my big brother very much. This was when I started considering myself an only child. So, having nothing better to reply with, I gave him the answer that a lot of kids give every day: "I don't know."

1980 | Secret Eating and Kiddie City

In the spring of third grade, Mom decided that I was mature enough to stay home alone after school. I became a latchkey kid who had a list of chores that better be done before she came home. I was given strict orders to do my chores and homework, stay in the apartment, and not answer the door. Since I was not supposed to go outside or have friends over, I did a half-assed job with my chores and then turned on the TV. This was before cable. So, I had to find a station with cartoons and then move the antenna around until the static cleared enough for me to see Hercules or Deputy Dog.

At some point, usually during a commercial, I made a snack. I didn't reach for fruit, even though we usually had apples and bananas on hand — not bad for a single-parent household. I would eat things that are gross to me now and should have been gross to me then. Once, I grabbed a cold hot dog out of the fridge and sat on the floor in front of the TV, just munching away. Most of the time, I ate a huge bowl of peanut butter Cap'n Crunch or Fruity Pebbles cereal.

One afternoon, after learning about protein, or "muscle meat" in health class, I grabbed a leftover cooked chicken leg and ate it cold, with my hands, over the sink. It was like I was in a zombie trance: "Must eat muscle meat!" On another day, I tried to make cornmeal mush after seeing it on a cartoon. Since I didn't live in the Deep South and I couldn't Google the recipe, I dumped cornmeal, flour, salt, and milk in a frying pan with melted butter. Boy, was that a nasty snack. I ate it right over the frying pan; it was salty and carby, so it was good to me. I started eating cookie dough about that time, too, sometimes homemade, but mostly the Pillsbury kind in the roll, if we had some.

I liked being alone; it was the only time I really felt safe in our apartment, but I didn't want to be home alone every day. I got lonely. My friend Jenny told me about this awesome place she went to after school to take dance lessons.

Jenny took ballet and tap dance lessons after school at this place called Kiddie City. She even got to ride in a van from Colbert to Kiddie City. One day, after I had begged her, my mom let me go with Jenny to take a free dance class. They let kids take one trial class to see if they liked it and really wanted to take lessons. I was so excited when I saw the Kiddie City van waiting in front of Colbert. We walked over to the van and I sat by Jenny so proudly. It was like we were going on an adventure. The van had no AC, even though it was South Florida. I was so thirsty, and I wished I had stopped at the water fountain on the way out of our classroom. The windows were all open and the warm wind made a mess of our hair, but we didn't care. That day, we sweated to death on the way to the daycare center and loved every minute of it.

All of the sweating and thirst was worth it. I LOVED that one dance class. We did both ballet and tap during that one lesson. Since I didn't have my own shoes, I had to borrow some, but I didn't care. I loved the sound the tap shoes made on the hardwood floor, and the ballet shoes made me feel like a real ballerina in my shorts and t-shirt. I did ballet moves with the rest of the class to "Here Comes the Sun" by the Beatles. After that, I wanted to come back twice a week like Jenny did, but the lessons were expensive, as were the clothes and shoes for the class. Mom couldn't swing the cost. So, I didn't end up taking a dance class until high school, when I took two years of dance as a PE elective for free. Mom ended up sending me to Kiddie City for summer camp one year, though. That was interesting.

The first thing I remember about Kiddie City summer camp is the half-popsicles. The camp director, or whoever did the shopping, would buy those cheap double popsicles but break them in half. It was always a big rush to get to where the counselor was handing out popsicles because I wanted one of the "good" colors, like red or purple. Orange was also acceptable. I hated the green ones. They reminded me of frogs, and I have always been afraid of frogs.

Most of the time, my mom packed my lunch during camp. When we were out of lunch meat or peanut butter, she sometimes made me hard-fried egg sandwiches. The yolk always looked green by lunchtime. Back in the day, we didn't use cute little blocks of ice. Lunch just sat in your Star Wars or Muppet metal lunch box or plain paper bag until lunchtime. You ate it at room temperature and, most of the time, no one got sick. I don't remember ever getting sick from a green egg sandwich, but I got embarrassed. One boy saw the green yolk and started making fun of me. I don't remember what he said, but I remember him pointing out my green yolk to ALL of the other boys. Boys always made me feel way more embarrassed than girls. I asked my mom if I could buy lunch at camp after that.

When you paid for lunch at camp, you had to order a half sandwich or a whole sandwich. I usually asked for a whole sandwich because, like adult Lisa, kid Lisa was always HUNGRY. One time, the counselor had a group of us around her near the basketball court. She was taking our lunch orders, and of course, there was a group of boys. Ugh. I had already been called fat and made fun of for eating a green egg. So, in my eight-year-old mind, I had to be dainty with my sandwich order. When the counselor called my name, I said, "Half."

That day, we were going to the skating rink for a field trip. So, the camp was bringing our sandwiches with us. We bought drinks at the rink. We skated for an hour, and then we all wheeled over to the snack bar area to pick up our sandwiches and drinks. The skating rink on Johnson Street was crappy and dark, with gross, dirty outdoor carpet in the snack bar area. I ignored all of this and focused on getting food because, as usual, I was STARVING.

It was tuna salad day. I'd recently realized that I liked mayonnaise and tuna salad. So, I took advantage of the darkness of the skating rink and took a whole sandwich. I sat down, far away from the boys, and began devouring my precious tuna sandwich. I was about halfway done when the counselor started asking if anyone "had taken a whole sandwich instead of a half." I kept my mouth shut and kept chewing. I was down to a half sandwich with a couple of bites taken out by then. The boy who got stuck with a half sandwich was mad, but I did not care.

As if it weren't stressful enough dealing with boys and sandwiches, I also had to take swimming lessons at Kiddie City. I had started fearing the water at a young age. Water is still not my favorite. My mom couldn't swim and she didn't want me to be like her, so she paid extra for private swimming lessons. I flat-out sucked at them.

The thing I hated most about swimming lessons was putting my face in the water and blowing bubbles. Ever the germophobe, I used to imagine how many kids had peed in the water whenever I had to put my face in it. Also, I hated that whole bubble-blowing thing they make kids do during swimming lessons. I would sometimes manage to get water up my nose while unsuccessfully blowing out. When I did blow out, I would end up with boogers hanging out of my nose. I rarely realized this until, of course, a boy pointed it out, loudly, in front of other boys.

I never learned to swim that summer, and I wouldn't for a few more years until I learned from a friend. I stopped going to Kiddie City after that summer. I spent the next couple of summers home alone or hanging out with Fran and Nicole. Kiddie City was too expensive.

1980 : Lesbian Landlady and the Shack of Roaches

When I was nine and in fourth grade, my mother attempted to become independent from her Rod. Rod was helping her pay the rent and other bills, so she kept him around even though he was married and he beat her. My mom thought if we got a cheaper place to live, we could get away from Rod. She decided we would move from our two-bedroom, two-bathroom duplex to an efficiency with no stove or living room. It was basically a master bedroom with a kitchen sink and a tiny refrigerator, and it was attached to the landlady's house.

Moving day wasn't as tough as it could have been if Mom hadn't convinced Rod to help us move. We had been wrapping our dishes and my mom's large knick-knack collection in the Hollywood Sun-Tattler and putting everything in liquor boxes that we had gotten from behind the liquor store. Rod came over after he went fishing with his son.

Rod carried all the boxes to my mom's car and his car and into the efficiency with sweat rolling down his face and coating his black hair. He smelled like beer and Old Spice when he sweat. We didn't have any furniture of our own, so after he carried in the boxes, he left us to unpack. It was already dark, so we unpacked what we needed to get ready for bed.

That night, the landlady used her key to open the door between her house and our tiny efficiency. I was in the bathroom when this happened. I didn't see anything. I just remember hearing my mom yell. It was a combination of her angry yell and her scared yell. Then, I heard the door slamming.

I asked my mother what happened and she told me the truth. She said the landlady was drunk and that she was a lesbian. My mom told me she had "made a pass" at her. She didn't give me the specifics on what went down during said pass, but I knew enough from watching TV to get the general idea. Apparently, the landlady wanted to take Rod's place.

Determined to keep any more unwelcome guests out of our place, Mom barricaded our door with every suitcase and box we'd brought with us. This time, key or not, the landlady would not be coming in so easily. It was already dark, and we had nowhere else to go, so we slept in the efficiency that night. During the night, I had to get up to go to the bathroom. That's when I saw the roaches. They were all over the walls and tub. They scattered, like roaches do, when I turned on the light. I screamed, and my mother came in. She let loose with a string of drunken sailor talk and said we were going to leave in the morning. And we did.

Rod wasn't truly out of the picture yet. After all, he helped us move. I don't think he understood my mom's intentions. Or maybe he knew that our time at our new "home" wouldn't be long. When my mom called him from the pay phone on the corner, he came back the next day and helped us move back to the duplex on Taylor Street. Yep. One night of a handsy landlady and a tub full of roaches was all it took to send us running back to Rod and the higher rent on Taylor Street.

The Friday before we moved for a day, I'd said goodbye to my classmates in Mrs. Baxter's class at Colbert Elementary. I'd told them I was moving and would have to go to Hollywood Central since that was the school near my new home. I remember the teacher asking me if I liked my new home. Not wanting to admit that we were moving to a one-room apartment that could only be entered through the backyard, I answered "It's okay." She took that as me not wanting to move. Like most teachers, she thought I was an average kid who lived in a house with an average family. She couldn't have been more wrong.

We moved back to our duplex apartment on Sunday. Monday morning, I was back in my seat in Mrs. Baxter's classroom talking to a couple of classmates who didn't make fun of my clothes or my mom's rusted-out Chevy. When Mrs. Baxter saw me, she did a double take.

"What happened? I thought you moved?" She asked.

"My mom changed her mind," I said, shrugging. That was the reason I gave. It was kind of true. I left out the part about the roaches, the landlady hitting on Mom, and her beer-scented boyfriend helping us move twice.

1980 | Orange Trees and Miss Kitty

Not only was I home alone every day after school, but I was also home alone if I had to stay home sick with something like a cold. Mom would leave my medicines on the nightstand next to my bed and call and check on me from work. Since she was a single mom, she couldn't stay home every time I was sick. So, I learned how many orange Coricidin pills or little cups of grape Tylenol to take. The stuff tasted good, but I knew that taking too much wasn't a good idea. I got tired of being inside. So, I figured that since the yard was sorta part of the apartment, going outside for a few minutes would be okay. So, I would walk out and pick some oranges. It was a lot less boring than watching TV or doing homework.

    The yard was full of orange trees, but it also had a lot of stickers, not the fun grape-scented kind, but the kind that stuck in your skin and hurt to pull out. Since I ran around in my flip-flops, or zories as Fran called them, I had these tiny green maces stuck in my feet and the bottom of my cheap shoes. I made sure to pick them off of my shoes and feet before going back in. I'd be in trouble if my mom stepped on one inside.

    After getting through the sticker field, a new challenge presented itself. The orange trees had a lot of spider webs in them, which housed small, hard spiders. I knew this because they crunched when I stepped on them with my flimsy shoes. A couple of times, I put my arm through a web while trying to get a free snack. I wasn't afraid of spiders, and I'm still not. If I see one in my house now, I will usually name it Fred and leave it be. They don't live long, and they are not there to hunt people, anyway. Now, if one jumped on me, I would probably not enjoy it.

Spiders weren't the only critters in the yard. There were also a few stray cats. I loved cats. Even at eight, I'd rather spend time with animals than people. They just seemed more honest. The cats killed lizards and birds, but they didn't try to befriend the smaller creatures before they took them down. They went after them with claws and teeth out right from the get-go. I admired them.

Most of the cats wouldn't let me near them. I understood this because, by eight, I had been sexually, physically, and emotionally abused. I knew humans could be complete garbage to their fellow living things. I didn't chase the cats. I just sat in any stickerless patch of grass I could find, ate my orange, and watched them hunt. One of them was brave, though. She came up to me and sniffed me. This is how I met Miss Kitty. I often wonder if I found Miss Kitty or if she found me. It didn't matter. We loved each other from the start. She was a young tiger-striped girl, full of energy. I hated that she lived outside. So, since I was home alone and my mom was at work, I brought Miss Kitty into our apartment and played with her. I gave her a bowl of water and some cheese, which she appreciated.

When my mom got home, she explained that Miss Kitty would need to be an outside pet. We weren't allowed to have a cat in our apartment, and Mom didn't want a litter box to deal with. So, we bought some Meow Mix and some Tender Vittles, and Miss Kitty came in and out throughout the day. I never really enjoyed letting her out, though, and I was always worried about her.

Soon after we adopted her, we figured out that Miss Kitty was going to be a mama kitty. So, we let her stay inside more, and mom caved and got a litter box, with the stipulation that I had to scoop it. I was eight; I could handle this. So, we left Miss Kitty inside all day long while Mom and I went to work and school.

One day, when we got home, Miss Kitty wanted to go outside. I picked her up before letting her out, but I noticed she was skinny. I yelled for my mom to tell her about the newly slender cat. My mom knew exactly what had happened. She went into my room and checked the closet and under my two twin beds. She found the four kittens under the twin bed by the window. They were so cute. There were two gray tigers and two orange tigers. It was almost like they had two different fathers, as there was one orange tom and one gray tom outside. Of course, I wanted to keep all the kittens.

We didn't keep the kittens long. I guess it was somewhere between eight and ten weeks, my mom asked me if I would rather keep a kitten or Miss Kitty. She said I could not keep all of them. I chose Miss Kitty. So, one day, when I came home from school, the kittens were gone. I was told that they all went to live on a farm in Davie, a rural part of South Florida. I have never believed this, though. I think they went to the animal shelter.

Shortly after the kittens found a new home, we moved from the duplex to a rental house a few miles away on Wilson Street. We brought Miss Kitty with us, and she remained an indoor-outdoor cat there, as well. She went out at night and came home in the morning.

Since she spent so much time outside, of course Miss Kitty got fleas and she brought them into our house. I was the first to notice because there were little spots of blood on my windowsill right next to my bed. Then, I saw that Miss Kitty was scratching a lot. I tried to wipe her down with a wet washcloth. In my mind, she just needed a bath.

Then, one Friday evening, when Mom was reading the *Enquirer* on the couch, she yelled, "FUCK!" I jumped, thinking she was going to hit me or throw things at me. Instead, she walked over with her index finger pointing out from her palm. "LOOK AT THIS! A FUCKING FLEA!"

I was so scared that my mom would get rid of Miss Kitty because she had fleas. I started crying and promised to give Miss Kitty a real bath with my shampoo. Mom told me that was a "stupid fucking idea, and it wouldn't work." The next morning, Mom called the vet and got Miss Kitty booked for a flea dip. Then, she bought three flea fogger "bombs" and put one in the living room and one in each of our bedrooms. She also got a flea collar for Miss Kitty. That seemed to do the trick, and all was well with Miss Kitty for a while.

When I was eleven, and in the beginning of my sixth-grade year, Mom and I moved again. This time to a duplex on 24th Avenue and Filmore Street. Once again, Miss Kitty got used to her life as an indoor-outdoor cat. She got to know the neighborhood and always came home — except when she didn't.

After we lived in our new duplex for a couple of months, Miss Kitty started acting weird, and she didn't come home for three days. I went out every day, shaking a bag of cat treats and calling for her. I walked up and down the alley behind our house, yelling, "HERE, KITTY KITTY!" Finally, one day, she came home. She looked different, though, skinnier and worn. When I tried to feed her, she refused to eat. I was crying because I was so worried about her, and even my mom looked concerned. She told me we would take her to the vet. Mom put Miss Kitty in a Snoopy pillowcase, which was our cat carrier, and we took her in the next day.

The vet's first course of action was to give Miss Kitty steroids, which, of course, increased her appetite and made her eat like a horse. I was thrilled because I thought this meant she was getting better. We kept her entirely inside during this time so we could monitor her. Mom and I noticed that Miss Kitty was not pooping. Shortly after that, she stopped eating again. We took her back to the vet for her final vet visit. The vet informed us that Miss Kitty had feline leukemia, a disease that outdoor cats often catch. He recommended we put her to sleep. My mom called him a quack for giving our cat steroids and giving us hope that she would recover. She was so mad, and I was just sad.

Miss Kitty was put to sleep while wrapped in my Raggedy Ann doll blanket. When we got to the check-out counter after Miss Kitty was gone, my mom refused to pay the bill, calling the doctor a "fucking con artist." I was so sad, and Mom just seemed angry. I cried for days after Miss Kitty was gone. I felt guilty about letting her stay outside. I should've snuck her in my window and kept her safe. I still tear up a little when I think of her and think of how much better her life would have been if my mom had let me keep her inside. As an adult, I have welcomed a few cats into my home over the years, and I never let them go outside because I don't want them to suffer like Miss Kitty did.

1981 | Prime Rib Breakfasts and Rubik's Cube Dreams

"You never had PRIME RIB?!" Terri, my friend from YMCA camp, yelled with her head in her refrigerator, and only her dark curls and Smurf pajamas were visible to me. Her parents were still asleep, and she was searching for something we could have for breakfast instead of cereal. And she had struck gold — her parents' leftovers from their date the night before.

I had spent the night at her house in Emerald Hills, and her parents had gone out to dinner the night before and left us with her older brother and a babysitter. Sitting on the real leather sofa in her family room that morning, I felt a little like I wanted to be adopted and a little like I just wanted to go home to the cut-up rental house on Wilson Street, where we had moved after we left the Taylor Street duplex for good, and make instant Cream of Wheat. I wanted to belong with Terri's family, but I just didn't feel like I did. I was amazed that Terri wanted to be my friend at all.

When I first met Terri I didn't think she would like me because she was one of the Pix soda girls at the YMCA summer camp. They were the affluent girls at camp who had an unlimited supply of sodas and made fun of my orange water wings and my blubber. Even though Terri was accepted by the Pix Soda crew with her thin frame, bikini, and cooler full of soda, she was not mean like the other girls. Terri had everything going for her in my eyes. Yet, she chose to befriend the awkward, fat, non-swimming girl who was surviving on one Capri-Sun a day and water from the rusty fountain near Pavilion 10 at TY Park.

One day, we were sitting at one of the picnic tables in Pavilion 10 and Terri handed me a torn half of her Fruit Roll-up. "Hey, do you wanna sleepover on Saturday?" she asked me. I finished chewing the red faux fruit, swallowed it with my last gulp of Capri-Sun, and said, "Okay. I have to ask my mom."

Somehow, I got my mom to talk to her mom on the phone and agree to let me sleep over. Maybe she needed some private time with Rod, or maybe the fact that they lived in Emerald Hills, which was one of the best neighborhoods in Hollywood, made her feel good about me spending time there. Whatever the reason, I was allowed to occupy Terri's trundle bed for one night. I got to cuddle her koala bear stuffed animal and play with her Rubik's Cube. And I got to eat prime rib for breakfast. It all felt so normal, and I knew I did not come from a normal family. I felt kind of sad when I had to go home, but I also felt a little relieved to be in my own room again.

When summer ended and we went back to our separate schools, Terri and I didn't see each other much. We talked on the phone, but it wasn't the same as sitting in the humidity and enjoying fake fruit products. Then, she called me on my birthday. I didn't think I'd ever see Terri in person again, but Terri told me that she and her mom were coming over to bring me a birthday gift. I wasn't having a party or anything. She just remembered that it was my birthday!

They arrived that afternoon, and I let them in. I walked Terri and her mom through the sunroom and past the unusable cricket-infested front bathroom into the dark living room. We sat on the ripped black vinyl couch and my mom came up the two steps and through the hanging black and red beads from her room. She fake smiled and looked at them and the gift bag I was holding.

I pulled the Koala out of the bag first. "Oh my god! It's just like yours! Thank you!" I hugged Terri.

"There's something else in there," her mom said quietly from her spot at the opposite end of the couch.

I reached in and pulled out my very own Rubik's Cube. "THANK YOU! I've always wanted one of these! Mom! Look!" I started unboxing it immediately.

My mom said, "Wow! Nice!" She looked at Terri's mom, trying to maintain her smile, and said, "You didn't have to do that." Adult Lisa understands that my mother felt inadequate at that moment because she did not have the money to buy these cool gifts. Kid Lisa thought that was a weird thing to say to someone who gave me birthday presents. Of course people should buy me birthday presents, especially rich people, and at that time I believe Terri's family was rich because they lived in a house that didn't have apartments attached to it and they had central air conditioning.

Terri and her mom didn't stay long. I don't blame them. The one-window air conditioner could not keep up with the South Florida September humidity. Once they went home, I went to my room and played with my Rubik's cube while holding my new koala in my lap. I was hoping I would get to go to Terri's again soon, but I never saw Terri again.

1981 | Fifth Grade Spy

"Put your tape recorder in here!" Mom said as she shoved a blue vinyl zippered bank bag into my lap. She had a couple of those lying around because her employer, a plastic surgeon, entrusted her with making the cash deposit every day. It wouldn't take long for my mom's boss to realize that trusting my mom with anything — let alone cash — was not a wise choice.

I sat on the ripped black vinyl couch in our dark living room at the carved-up multi-rental house on Wilson Street, and I shoved the cassette tape recorder I had gotten for Christmas into the bag. It was a tight fit, but I got it in and managed to zip it. My first tape recorder/player was NOT a cute little Walkman; it was an 11 x 6 generic Radio Shack hunk of black plastic, and I loved it. I created my mini talk shows before anyone knew what a podcast was. It was a talk show with zero listeners, but I still enjoyed creating it.

Today was not about fun, though. Today was about getting evidence against "that son of a bitch who sold me this piece of shit Sunbird," according to my mom. She wanted to "sue their asses" and make lots of money. "Their asses" were those that belonged to the "motherfuckers" who worked at the Hollywood Ford car dealership. I wonder why I have such a potty mouth. Profanity was practically my first language. I think my mom counted this as one of our "You and Me Against the World" activities that she learned about from popular singer Helen Reddy.

I liked the cute blue Sunbird. It was the first non-embarrassing car she'd owned in my lifetime. The one before it was that green, dull, rusted clunker that she must've floated a check for. I hated being driven to school in that thing. All the kids made fun of me, especially when I walked from the car to the building wearing knock-off sneakers that I got from Pantry Pride.

The Sunbird was different. It was shiny, dark blue, and had tiny racing stripes down the sides. It was as cool as a four-door car could be in the early 80s. It had a little habit of conking out when we were on our way somewhere. Mom and I had spent some time walking home from various places because Sunny (that was the car's name) had a tummy ache, which was my professional diagnosis.

Lucky for us, the car was running on spy mission day. I hopped in the front passenger seat, and Mom took the wheel. She backed out of our grassy parking spot in front of the house and headed down Federal Highway to Hollywood Ford. On the way, I had to take the recorder out and reposition it in the vinyl bag so that the small, square microphone was near where the zipper opened. I was going to get this car-slinging con artist on tape. I had no clue what Mom would actually do with the tape; I just knew I had to sit next to her and look like a normal, innocent kid holding a bank bag and hide my true identity as Mama's spy.

Mom pulled into the Hollywood Ford parking lot and parked near the building. I reached my hand into the vinyl bag and pushed the record and play buttons at the same time. She picked up her purse and told me to pretend the bank bag was my purse. So, I carried it under my arm and followed Mom. Of course, one of the salesmen came up to her immediately. She told them she wanted to talk to the sales manager. Mom was pulling a Karen before that was even a thing. For her, it was a normal Janet thing to do.

We were led to an office with two blue plastic chairs and some gray-haired guy behind a desk. I sat in the one closest to the wall and double-checked the zipper opening on my "purse." Then I sat there quietly, nodded, and smiled politely when the sales manager said hello to me.

Mom started in on the dude immediately. She told him about the many times Sunny the Sunbird had stalled in the middle of busy streets and how dangerous that was. Mom let him know that she was a single mom and needed a reliable car to get to work. She demanded a refund or a different car because they had sold her a lemon. Mom kept trying to get the guy to admit that they knew it was a bad car when they sold it. I don't think he ever did, but I had my recorder ready just in case.

Mom ended the conversation by getting up abruptly and telling the guy to bend over so she could "drive the damn car up his fucking ass!" He did not oblige. He kept saying, "Janet, we'll fix it! Just leave it with us." She didn't. Well, not on that day. The Sunbird was in to be fixed many times after this meeting.

Four years later, Mom married my stepdad and cashed in her 401K for a Cadillac. She gave the Sunbird to my brother, Tony, but he didn't keep it long. He traded it in at a small used car lot on 441 for a car that ended up catching on fire.

1982 Yellow on the Fourth of July

I woke up in the early, dark hours of the morning. I had the worst stomach pain ever, only it was up high, almost in my chest. Since I was having chest pains, and since my father had already had a heart attack by this time, I ran into my mom's room and told her I was having a heart attack. I truly believed this. I was ten.

My mom brought me back to my room and told me I probably wasn't having a heart attack. She had me point to where my pain was and then brought the trash can closer when I announced I was going to barf. And I did. Then she had me brush my teeth and go back to bed. She gave me half of an Ativan to help me sleep. I am surprised she did because a day or two before, after I had gotten home from spending the night at Maryjane's house, she told me I looked yellow.

I first met Maryjane when I was about eight and lived on Taylor Street. Maryjane, her brother David, and her parents lived in the apartment behind Fran and Nicole. When they first moved in, I heard them before I saw them.

Maryjane's dad had a deep, growly Southern accent. "Murjane, Murjane. Git in here girl! Dyvid! Get over here; I'm gonna whoop you!" And whoop them he did. Maryjane's dad was fierce. I felt sorry for them as I could sometimes hear the "whoopins" when they left their front door open. They didn't live on Taylor Street for long. I'm pretty sure it was less than a year. After they moved out, I didn't see Maryjane for a while.

A couple of years later, when I was ten, I ran into Maryjane at Lincoln Park, which was two blocks from Taylor Street and a block down the street from the duplex we moved to after leaving the Taylor Street apartment. My mom and I moved a lot during the 70s and 80s, but we always stayed in East Hollywood.

Maryjane's new home was a tiny cottage that was nearly hidden under a gigantic tree. It was right across the street from the park and surrounded by other small homes with overgrown landscaping. My neighborhood wasn't exactly a Better Homes and Gardens kind of place.

So, since we lived close to each other again, Maryjane and I became the best of friends. Mom wasn't too happy about that as Maryjane was a couple of years older than me and was "white trash" according to my mom. When I begged her to let me sleep over at Maryjane's tiny cottage one night, Mom caved in and let me. In her defense, I pestered her a lot. Still, I have to say, as a parent, I never would have let my kid sleep there.

What a weird night it was. Right when my mom dropped me off, Maryjane told me we were going out on the town. By out on the town, she meant we were going to walk across the tracks and hang out at a laundromat where we could buy snacks from vending machines and talk to grown-ups doing their laundry or hanging out and drinking beer in the parking lot. Again, not a Better Homes and Gardens kind of hood.

In order to go out, we first had to get ready. Maryjane made me take a shower at her house. She didn't have shampoo because it was too expensive, so we washed our hair with watered-down dish soap. I am impressed that my hair did not fall out. After we stripped our hair of any oil, we used mousse and a curling iron to get our tresses into 1982 shape. We also used some makeup that was in the bathroom. At that point in my life, being barely out of fifth grade, I didn't question using someone else's makeup.

Once our hair and makeup were done, Maryjane insisted I wear one of her miniskirts. The green shorts I had on were unacceptable for "going out." I put on Maryjane's clothes and we walked out of the house, at night, by ourselves, and her parents were okay with this. I was thrilled but a little scared, too.

Our first stop was not the laundromat, but a local DJ's house down the street. I don't remember his name, and that is probably a good thing because he was a popular DJ on Y-100, the most popular pop station in South Florida. He was also in his 30s, and I found it odd that we were just going to visit a full-grown man. It got odder.

The DJ offered us marijuana and, being ten and scared, I said no. Both Maryjane and the DJ made fun of me for a bit. They called me a wimp and told me it was "only pot." I still said no. Then, the DJ asked me if I wanted to watch TV while he and Maryjane went into the bedroom "to talk." I was scared and speechless, so I just sat on the couch and watched TV while my twelve-year-old friend went into a man's bedroom who had just offered us drugs. I was starting to wish I could go home.

Eventually, Maryjane came out of that bedroom. It seemed like days, but it was probably more like an hour. She seemed okay. I don't remember if she told me what she did with him. She just told me it was no big deal. I told her I wanted to go home. She told me to go back to her house because she was going to the damn laundromat with or without me.

I did. I went to her house, where her parents and David were hanging out. I told the grownups about going to the DJ's house and Maryjane smoking pot. I also told them I wanted to call my mom and go home. They laughed at me and told me it was probably "just that homegrown stuff," and besides, it was "only pot." I slept on the couch that night and called my mom first thing in the morning. I was never so happy to see my mom arrive to pick me up from a friend's house. Usually, I wanted to stay longer. I never went back to Maryjane's house, and I didn't hang out with her much after that.

A couple of days after leaving her house, I was in the hospital with unbearable abdominal pain and yellow skin, which my mom had noticed earlier.

It was a Saturday afternoon, I was on the living room floor, coloring and watching TV. My mom was sitting on the loveseat reading tabloids when she asked me to walk over to her, where the light was brighter. She grabbed my chin, moved my face around, and said, "That's weird. You looked kind of yellow from over there." That was it. I guess I didn't look THAT yellow. I wasn't feeling bad at that point. So, Mom and I just went on doing our thing. Neither one of us thought there was anything wrong with me until I started having those "heart attack" pains days later.

After Mom gave me the Ativan, I went back to sleep and woke up the next morning feeling pretty normal. That morning was the Fourth of July. So, I didn't have to go to school, and mom didn't have to go to work. We decided to go out to breakfast at our favorite place — Wags. I was hungry, so I ordered French Toast and bacon, which was my favorite item on the menu. Now that I'm a grown-up and understand what I had going on health-wise, I know that bacon was not the best thing to order.

I wolfed down that greasy bacon. I loved it. I felt okay for a bit after eating it until we got to the local grocery store, Pantry Pride. We were almost done with our shopping. In fact, we were on the last aisle, the frozen foods aisle. Mom had just put some sort of frozen Salisbury steak dinner in the cart when I announced that my heart attack had returned.

My mom turned to look at me and asked, "Is this a heart attack where I can finish shopping and take the groceries home, or is this the kind of heart attack where we leave the cart right here and head to the hospital?" I chose option B. I was in horrible pain, and I felt like I would throw up again. True to her word, Mom left the full cart right there, grabbed her purse, and grabbed my hand. Off we went.

We got to Memorial Hospital within ten minutes. Mom and I walked into the emergency room, and she told them I was having chest pains and that my father had a heart attack recently. They got me in a bed quickly and hooked me up to an EKG machine. That was a little uncomfortable because the gel they used with the electrodes was cold. Also, I was just starting puberty, so I was embarrassed when they started putting electrodes on my chest.

It only got more uncomfortable from there. Once they determined I was not having a heart attack, the other tests started. My chest pain gradually got worse.

The hospital staff put me in a room with three other patients and their moms. One of the girls had eaten an entire bottle of her uncle's lithium because it looked like M and M candies. They had pumped her stomach, and she was sleeping when I first got to my bed. Her family was standing around her.

This was my first time in the hospital, and I didn't know what to expect. Soon after I got undressed and into my hospital gown, a nurse came over and closed the curtain around my bed. My stomach started hurting, along with my chest. The nurse inserted an IV in my hand and took blood from my arm while telling my mom, "We can't give her anything for the pain because we don't know what she has."

My mom got mad at the nurse for not helping me with the pain. One of the other moms in the room saw how angry my mom was getting and offered to help. She taught me Lamaze breathing. She explained to me that Lamaze breathing was something that pregnant women did when they were in labor to deal with the pain. This other mom had me stare at the blinking light on my IV and breathe slowly. It worked for a bit. I stopped doing Lamaze when the fireworks started, though. I felt well enough to wheel my IV over to the window to see them.

I was in the hospital for three days, and the doctors ordered all kinds of tests to figure out why I was having this pain. I was also on a restricted diet of clear liquids. The worst test they did was some sort of kidney test. The technicians had me lie on a metal table, and they injected a huge amount of fluid into my IV. Then, when my bladder was full, they started scanning my abdomen. They pushed down hard with whatever machine they were using. I don't think it was an x-ray, but I can't be certain. It was torture. When they were finally done, they let me go to the bathroom. Sweet relief! One tech told me she was proud of me for not peeing on the table. She said that some grownups had peed themselves during this test. I can see why. And it was all for nothing. My kidneys were fine.

Finally, one of the tests gave them useful results, and the doctors finally figured out what was wrong with me. I had hepatitis A. We were told that I could have caught it anywhere, possibly in a restaurant. Basically, if someone has hepatitis A and uses the bathroom and doesn't wash their hands, they can pass it on by touching food or other items. Gross, right? Mom immediately thought that I caught hepatitis from Maryjane's house, where I had spent the night earlier that week. While I have no proof, I don't disagree with her. From what I saw, they were really worried about hand washing there.

Once they figured out what I had, they let me start eating again. First, it was just creamy soups. Then, other bland foods were added. Finally, on my last day in the hospital, I was allowed to order food from the menu. Only, since they were sending me home, I wasn't going to eat dinner there. I was really disappointed because I wanted to order regular food. Mom told me not to worry about that, and she would get me something from Burger King. I wasn't having it. I wanted to eat hospital food. My mom must have felt sorry for me because she asked the nurse if I could check out after dinner. I was thrilled when I got to circle things on the menu. I ordered lamb and mint jelly with apple juice and a cookie for dessert. It sounded fancy, but everything except the cookie tasted terrible. I regretted turning down Burger King.

1982 | Dull Not Shiny

"Why's your clarinet so old and ugly?" Seth said to me while I was attempting to play a higher-octave warm-up scale before band class.

I stopped playing and looked up from my blue band book. I turned my head to the left to look at Seth, but quickly looked away from his face and up at his hair. I stared at his curly brown hair, avoiding his eyes, which always looked mean to me. Seth was one of the rich kids, and I was not. He had the right clothes: Jordache, Sergio Valente, Osh Kosh, Ocean Pacific, and Members Only. Most kids had all the new, popular stuff I didn't have. I got most of my clothes from Sears or Lerner's. We couldn't even afford to buy underwear at Burdines or Macy's, where the rich kids shopped.

"Your clarinet's all old and gross. Even the case is all rusted and stuff. Why didn't you just get a normal clarinet, like everyone else?" Seth looked at me, and I looked down at my clarinet, not knowing what to say.

I looked back at my music book and then across to the saxophone section, where Mr. Ratliff was helping Bob with his solo. I could feel my face heat up a bit, and I felt my stomach start to hurt. I looked back at Seth's wild, curly hair and said, "I don't know." Then, I put my clarinet in my mouth, licked the reed, and continued to warm up. The reed still tasted like cinnamon Binaca, my favorite. All the clarinet players sprayed Binaca on their reeds; it made them taste a little better, which helped because we had to lick them constantly. Seth started talking to the girl next to him, Kim, a skinny, red-headed girl with super short hair. She always laughed really loud and had the worst breath, but she had the right clothes, and her parents had the right car, so the prep crew accepted her. Kim and Seth were talking about my clarinet. I pretended not to hear and kept playing.

Mr. Ratliff returned from helping Bob. He tapped on the top of the podium and raised his hands to conduct. This was our cue to bring our instruments to our mouths and get ready to play. We were working on "Late in the Evening" by Paul Simon. I didn't like Paul Simon that much; I always confused him with Paul McCartney, who my mom and my Fran loved. They even thought that Mr. Ratliff looked like Paul McCartney. I didn't think so because Paul McCartney smiled. Mr. Ratliff was always yelling at us because we were not in tune. One time, he stopped the whole band and made me tune my clarinet. I thought for sure that my head was going to catch on fire from embarrassment. I felt like everyone in the whole band was laughing at me, even though the room was quiet.

I looked to the right, at the first and second chair clarinet players, and left at Seth, Kim, and the other 15 players before we started playing again. The first section of clarinets had the melody in this song, so we didn't start playing until the fourth or fifth measure. Seth was right. I was the only person in the clarinet section with a dull clarinet. Everyone else had the same shiny Bundy clarinets with the shiny new cases, not that I hadn't noticed this since the beginning of the year when I started in band. I didn't fit in. Everyone else was happy to be there, and it seemed like everyone else played better. I felt like I was always squeaking, even when I played a G, which was the easiest note to play. I would've quit band if my mom had let me, but she wouldn't. She had just paid off my clarinet, so I had to play it for at least another year.

Somehow, I managed to get third chair. I think it's because I cried during chair tryouts, and Mr. Ratliff felt sorry for me. I hate that I cried. It was so embarrassing, and Seth made fun of me for a week. He would fake cry every day, in band and at lunch. I didn't even want to play the clarinet. On the first day of band, when

Mr. Ratliff asked us what we wanted to play, I told him I wanted to play the recorder. No, not a tape recorder, but the instrument we played in music class in elementary school. I loved playing the recorder, and I already owned one, but I couldn't play it in band because it was "not a band instrument," according to Mr. Ratliff. That made no sense to me because it sounded like a flute to me, and a flute is a band instrument.

Since I liked the recorder and all, Mr. Ratliff made me try the flute; but, I couldn't make a sound with it. My lips were kind of big and they didn't go into that bird-mouth position well. So, I picked the only other "girl" instrument, the clarinet.

My mom had always wanted to play the clarinet, and she was thrilled that I was doing something she actually wanted me to do. I was happy that she was happy for once because she always seemed to be angry. Anyway, she had saved up some money so that we could go to the school on the night that the instrument store would be there to rent instruments. I remember I was so excited to finally get my clarinet. That's when everyone in the beginning band got instruments.

We never made it to school that night. Instead of getting me a shiny new Bundy clarinet, my mom decided to try to kill herself instead.

1982 | Open Psych

What was odd about the whole situation was that my mom was actually in a good mood that night. She came home from work looking sort of soft and happy instead of angry and stressed. She was peaceful. Normally, as soon as she got home, she yelled at me for not doing my chores right, or for having Miss Kitty in the house. I was supposed to vacuum, dust, clean my room, and make dinner before she got home, depending on what day it was. Some days, I vacuumed and dusted. Others, I cleaned my room. I made dinner often, too. I usually put raw chicken in a baking pan and poured a bunch of barbeque sauce all over it. Then, I would put it in the oven for like an hour. Dinner was ready when she got there, usually.

I didn't make dinner that night since we had to go to rent my clarinet. We were going to have a can of soup before going to school. I expected my mom to be angry about having to go somewhere at night. She liked to put on her pajamas and watch TV after work. So, I expected her to be all pissed off, but she was weird, like happy, but in a quiet way.

As soon as Mom got through the door, she hugged me and told me what a good daughter I was. This was weird because I forgot to vacuum. I was watching an after-school special about a girl who jumped off a building after doing angel dust, so it kind of held my attention. I was worried about the girl on TV, not our crappy beige carpet.

After my mom finished hugging me, she told me to ride my bike to Fran's house to get something for her. It wasn't far, and I loved getting out of the house. Mom told me that Fran would give me a bag and to hold it carefully. When I got to Fran's house, I grabbed the bag in a hurry, and I didn't even stop to pet her cats and dog or to say hi to Nicole. Normally, I loved to spend time with Fran and Nicole. I especially loved her pets, but I had to hurry because we needed to get to the band room to get my clarinet.

I figured out that there was a bottle of wine in the bag as soon as Fran gave it to me. I had to ride one-handed so that I could hug the paper bag in one arm. I knew if I dropped it and broke the bottle, I would get a few choice words and objects thrown in my direction. Mom was a screamer and a thrower. So, I held the wine like it was a baby and pedaled home as fast as I could. It seemed kind of odd that my mom sent me to get wine because she wasn't a drinker. Plus, she had to drive soon. I didn't ask my mom many questions, though. I just did what I was told and brought the wine home.

When I got home, my mom was in the bathroom. I could hear the medicine cabinet open and the water running in the sink. Our apartment was pretty small compared to a normal house. It had two bedrooms and one bathroom. Compared to the other kids, I didn't have the "right house" either. That's why I rarely had anyone come over.

I heard pills being poured out of a bottle, and then I heard more water running. I put the wine on the kitchen table and started to cook some chicken noodle soup on the stove. I looked at the clock on the wall and saw it was almost time to leave. My mom was still in the bathroom, so I kept getting dinner ready. She still wasn't out when the soup was done. I set the table and put a lid on the pan. I walked back to the closed bathroom door and knocked.

"What, honey?" Mom answered but from her bedroom. She was lying down and talking on the phone.

I turned around to face her bedroom and said, "Um, dinner's ready," as quietly as I could, and looked down at the carpet.

"I'm not hungry. You eat," my mom said and then started talking again. "Gary, you still there," she said into the phone in a tired voice.

The only Gary I knew was my father, but my mom hardly ever talked to him. She hated him. He never picked me up when he said he would, and he didn't pay child support. I hardly ever visited him. This was fine with me because he used to hit my mom and stuff. I never saw it happen, but she told me that. I had seen Rod hit her, so I guessed this was something my mom put up with.

After my mom tried to kill herself, my dad took an interest in me again. Like everyone else on the planet, I have a biological father. I mean, duh, we all need TWO parents in order to become a person, right? But I use the word "parent" very lightly when it comes to my father. Really, "sperm donor who cheated on my mom and left for good when she was seven months pregnant" is more accurate.

I saw my father about five or ten times in my life. The few times I talked to my dad as a kid, I liked him. My mom always told me what a crappy husband he was, and I knew that he rarely visited me, but I still liked him. We seemed to share a dry, sarcastic sense of humor. He was intelligent, musical, and a little mystical. He read my Tarot cards and told me stories about the ghosts that haunted his house. I found him fascinating, and like all kids of divorce, I used to wish that my parents would be back together. It never happened.

I walked back to the kitchen and put some soup in a bowl. I ate a few bites, but I had lost my appetite. I was kind of nervous and nauseated. We were already late for instrument rental at the school, and my mom was just lying down. Plus, she was taking pills. She took a bunch of pills once before when I was in fifth grade. That time, Rod came over and made her vomit into the kitchen sink. It was really gross. He yelled at me to go to bed, so I went into my room and hid under the covers.

After mom finished puking, I heard him walk her to her room and close the door. Then, he came into my room and laid down next to me on my bed. I turned away from him and continued to pretend to sleep. He came closer and wrapped his arms around my waist. He whispered it was okay and kissed my head. I can't remember what happened after that, but I feel sick when I think about it.

Since the whole puke-in-the-sink episode wasn't so long ago, I was worried about my mom that night. I threw the soup away and cleaned the pan and bowl. I also wiped the counter and the table very carefully. One time, I forgot to clean up after dinner, and there was a small piece of wet cat food on the counter. Mom wiped it with her finger and licked it because she thought it was some of what she had cooked. She screamed at me when she realized it was cat food. After that, I wiped the counter a lot.

After cleaning, I went to my room, sat on my bed, and listened to the radio on my alarm clock. After Mom got off the phone with my dad, she came into my room. She stood in front of me, rocking back and forth and slurring her words. She told me I was going to be okay and not to be sad. I was confused and more than a little scared.

That's when the ambulance got there. I opened the door when the paramedics knocked. Since they had on their uniforms and I had heard the siren, I knew it was okay to let them in. They asked me where my mom was, and I took them to her room. I went back to my room and sat on the floor. I didn't feel good, but I didn't want to throw up. I sat there with my arms over my abdomen and tried not to think of how fast my heart was beating or how nauseated I was until the paramedics told me they were taking my mom to the hospital. I had to ride in the ambulance with them since I was only 11 and no one else was at home. I guess my dad had called the ambulance but was not coming to pick me up.

Sally Mitchell came to get me at the hospital. Mom would need to stay in the hospital, in the open psychiatric ward, because she had tried to harm herself, something she denied the rest of her life. My dad did not want to "babysit" me, so I had to stay with the Mitchells for a few days. In a way, I thought this was a good thing because the Mitchells were a nice family; they were normal, not like us. The only thing I didn't like was that they were also really religious. They went to a Baptist church, and they sometimes talked Mom into bringing me to church. I had to go to vacation Bible school over the summer one year, and I hated it. It was sort of good to get out of the house, but I was never interested in church. I was so bored and yawned whenever we went into the chapel. Something about the stale air and the super quietness that made me want to go to sleep. Plus, I had a hard time believing in God, Jesus, Mary, and all of that stuff. It just seemed like a Saturday morning cartoon. I never told this to Mike or Sally, the parents of the Mitchell family, because I was afraid they would get mad at me and tell me I was going to hell. I have no memory of them ever being mad at me, but I thought that grown-ups got mad at children because that is what my mom did. It seemed like she was always mad at me.

Walking into the Mitchell's house made me hungry. It always smelled like freshly baked bread, or bacon, or whatever Sally had made earlier in the day. The day I arrived from the hospital, it smelled like fried okra. Sally grew up in South Carolina and made the most delicious food. There were no fast food or TV dinners for the Mitchells or their guests.

Their home was cozy and small. They had three bedrooms, one converted from a garage, and one bathroom. Six people lived in this small house. The Mitchells had four kids, three boys and one girl. Kathleen was the girl, but everyone called her K.K. I was staying with her in her room. K.K. and I were happy about this and got right down to the business of being roommates. She was about three years younger than me, but we were still pretty good friends. She loved country music, especially Kenny Rogers. I was starting to like Duran Duran, but I was okay with Kenny, too. So,

K.K. put on a record, and Kenny's voice filled the room with "The Gambler." We knew all the words to the chorus, and we started singing:

You got to know when to hold 'em
Know when to fold 'em
Know when to walk away
And know when to run
You never count your money
When you're sittin' at the table
There'll be time enough for countin'
When the dealin's done.

K.K. and I got so into the song that we started dancing. We were holding hands, jumping and dancing in her room when her mom walked by the door and yelled, "WHAT ARE YOU DOING?"

I got scared because she sounded furious. I dropped K.K's hands and looked down at the floor. She answered her mother, "We were dancing."

"Kathleen Kay, you know better than that," Sally told her daughter. Then, she looked at me and said, "We don't dance like that in this house." She stared at me for a minute.

"Okay. Sorry." I stammered. My stomach hurt. I hoped she wouldn't hit me.

Sally stopped staring at me and walked out of the room to her room about four steps down the hall. After she left, two of K.K.'s brothers came into the room. Her youngest brother, Dave, was a few years older than me, and her oldest brother, Darrell, was about 19. Dave mentioned I was staying there with them for a bit, and K.K. said, "Yes, because her mom tried to kill herself." I remember feeling like I was going to cry. Until then, it hadn't occurred to me that that was what my mom was trying to do. I didn't think that she was actually trying to kill herself. I thought about what would happen to me if my mother died when Darrell's booming voice brought me out of my thoughts.

"Don't say that," he yelled at K.K.

K.K. stammered an apology, and I told her it was okay because it was the truth. My mom had tried to kill herself.

I only stayed at the Mitchells' house for a day or two. Maybe it was the dancing, or maybe they just didn't want a seventh person sharing their bathroom. Anyway, after that, I got to stay with Fran and Nicole, which is where I wanted to go.

Usually, in a situation like this, when one parent is in the hospital, the other parent takes over. My father was alive and well, but for whatever reason, he decided that if he didn't get to know me, he couldn't miss me. So, I rarely visited my dad, and I did not stay with him when my mother was in the hospital.

I enjoyed staying with Fran and Nicole because they were nicer than my mom. Fran was a relaxed mom. So, the atmosphere was calmer. My stomach didn't hurt so much. She never yelled at me, and I only remembered her being angry at me once when I was about five.

One day, when I was about five, I was hanging out at Fran's, and I got bored. I also was feeling angry at Pete because he frightened me. He didn't do anything bad to me; he was never really nice and yelled at the TV. I got a hold of some nail clippers, and I scratched "Pete" into the toilet seat. I'm not sure what made me do that, but it seemed like the right thing to do in my little brain because it would get Pete in trouble. It didn't. When Fran saw that, she got angry at me. She didn't hit me, but she yelled, and her face looked furious. I instantly regretted carving the toilet seat and making Fran angry.

So, that was the only time Fran had ever been angry at me when I was a child, and I deserved it. I always felt safe around her because she was normally a very mellow person. I was happy when I stayed at Fran's. I think Sally apologized that I couldn't stay with her family, and I may have pretended to be sad about that. Really, it was a giant relief to be in a house where it was okay to dance, and laugh, and start eating without praying first.

I think one reason Fran was so nice was because she didn't work outside her home; she didn't have the stress of dealing with other people. She stayed home and cared for Nicole and Pete. Fran also didn't stress about keeping a clean house like my mom did. She always had a lot of cats. Because of the cats, there was usually fur everywhere. Fran's house wasn't as bad as the houses on *Hoarders*, but it wasn't totally clean like my house always was. Instead of cleaning, Fran taught Nicole all the things she taught me when I was four. Nicole was really smart and had a great imagination, too.

While I was staying with Fran, she took me to visit my mom in the hospital. We sat in her room and talked to her about the hospital and when she was going to get out. They made her stay for about a week, or at least that's how long it seemed. The nurses and doctors forced my mom to socialize with the other patients, but she didn't like most of them. She thought she didn't belong there and had taken too many Ativan with wine by mistake because she was frustrated with not being able to pay the bills with only her salary. My mom made one friend at the hospital. I can't remember his name, but he was a young guy in his twenties who was in a wheelchair. He played the guitar. After my mom got out of the hospital, she would go visit him sometimes at the home he shared with his mom.

When we visited my mom, we would sit in her room on those ugly, green plastic chairs they have for visitors. Mom would sit on her bed. She and Fran would joke about how she was in the loony bin and all. I didn't think it was funny, and I would mostly just sit there with a huge stomachache and think about how my mom almost died. I would try to imagine living with my dad in Miami, and my stomach would hurt more. Not only did I not know my dad, but he lived in Miami, a big, scary city to me. When my mom had the news on, I would hear about shootings and riots in Miami. I didn't want to live there or go to school there. McNichol was bad enough. It was like a little piece of Miami in Hollywood.

Mom was on the first floor, which was "Open Psych." The second floor was "Closed Psych." The closed psychiatric ward was just that, closed. It was locked. The patients had to stay in their rooms.

It was where the most insane people were. The doctors and nurses told my mom that if she did not do well on the first floor, she would need to go "one floor up." For the longest time, that was a big joke. Whenever Mom, or Fran, me, or any friend who knew about the joke did anything odd, one of us would say, "Uh oh. You're going one floor up." Then everyone would laugh, even me. Really, I didn't think it was that funny. The thought of my mom being crazy, dead, or institutionalized frightened me. She was angry and didn't make the best decisions, but she was truly all I had. We didn't have family in Florida, other than Fran and Nicole, and they weren't related to us. We had Rod, but having him was scarier than having no one.

1982 | Hiding from Rod

Instinct told me to pull the short, thin blanket over my head and pretend to be asleep when I saw him walk in. My mother's abusive, alcoholic, married boyfriend, Rod, had just walked in the front door of the daycare center where he and my mom had dropped me off hours ago. The center was having a New Year's Eve sleepover for kids, and they decided I should stay there even though, at age 11, I felt like I could stay home alone at night. I'd been doing it during the day for three years.

The center itself wasn't so bad. They gave us junk food and let us watch the festivities in New York on TV. I remember dancing around and singing "I've Done Everything for You" with Rick Springfield. I pointed at other kids while I no doubt made neighborhood dogs wail from the sound of my "singing" voice. The other kids looked at me like the misfit I was. I stopped singing.

The staff finally made us go to bed or cot sometime after my performance. It was really late and very dark when Rod came into the center and started talking loudly to people at the front desk. I was frightened and wondered where my mother was and if she was okay.

Rod had already proven himself to be an all-around bad guy. He took us out to eat, which was cool, but he usually drove drunk there and back. Once, he dropped us off at the wrong duplex because he was so drunk. My mom yelled at him even though she knew he was drunk and could get violent. Rod had already dislocated her jaw once by this time. One of our neighbors must have heard my mom scream that time because the cops arrived shortly after Rod hit her.

The two officers stepped through the Florida room and into the living room, where my mom was seated in a chair in the corner. I sat on the side of the loveseat that was farthest away from my mom. I was nine, and I had been seeing my mother get beaten for three years at this point. It made me angry at her for staying with him and it made my stomach hurt something fierce. The cops stood next to my mom. One was asking her questions while the other took notes. They asked if she needed to go to the hospital, and she said she would go later. Besides declining medical care, like so many women, she also declined to press charges. Rod was back at our house within a week.

Rod didn't just hurt my mother. He hurt himself. One time, when they were arguing, he attempted to slit his wrists with my mom's razor. I can remember seeing pieces of skin and drops of blood in the sink before I was told to go to my room. The next time we saw Rod, he had large bandages on his wrists.

I don't think it's a coincidence that Rod's entrance into my life occurred at about the same time as my stomach issues began. I started to get terrible stomachaches every day. My mom just couldn't figure out what was wrong, so she took me to the doctor. He told her to watch what I was eating and to make sure I wasn't putting "too much goop" on my sandwiches. No one thought maybe it was stress-related. I understand that first-graders rarely have stressful lives, but I did.

The woman at the counter told Rod he could not take me. I couldn't hear her exact words from my cot, but when I peeked out from under my blanket, I could see that he was pointing toward the room of cots and seemed insistent on taking me home. She stood her ground and shook her head and put her hand out in front of her. I imagine he must have smelled like whiskey and beer, and he was probably belligerent. Whatever her reasons were, I'm grateful that the woman did not let Rod take me with him. Not only was he physically abusive to my mom and himself, but he did things to me, too.

When I got a little older, probably around ten, Rod got really weird with me. He would come over when my mom wasn't home. He had a key to our place, so he would just walk right in. If I were in my room with the door closed, he would just walk right in there, too. I can remember changing my clothes and having him walk right in. When I tried to cover up, he told me he had "seen it already."

This is also about the time that Rod started kissing me on the mouth and opening his mouth. I found this to be odd and uncomfortable, but I went along with it because I was afraid of him. Also, my mom had told me he helped her pay her bills, and that was why she kept him around. If I ruined that for her, she would be angry, and our electricity might be turned off again. I really hated cold baths and not having air conditioning, lights, hot food, or TV. I didn't tell my mother until I was twelve. She didn't break up with him until I was thirteen. I felt like he must have been more important to her than I was.

1982 | Merry Fucking Christmas!

Mom was even more anxious from Thanksgiving to Christmas. During a normal month, we were rolling coins from the piggy bank to pay rent. Add the extra shopping that comes with Christmas, and living on my mom's paycheck became impossible. That is where Rod came in.

It must have been easy to get someone a credit card on your account back in the 80s because my mom had a few cards with her first name and Rod's last name. Since he was married to someone else, I often wondered if his wife also had duplicate cards on his account. This was before the world was so computerized, so I can see how they got away with this. Maybe they could get away with it now, too, if the credit card company thought that Rod was some sort of rogue polygamist.

One Christmas season, my mom was super mad at Rod for something, probably for being married or for beating her again. This guy was a prize. Did I mention that? Anyway, she was super pissed and took all her fake Mrs. Rod cards shopping. We went everywhere using those cards. I remember seeing Rod's last name when my mom signed the imprinted 1980s credit card receipt. That was back when they had to make an actual imprint of the card on a three-ply carbon receipt.

As it got later in the day, and we were heading home, we had time for one last — Eckerd Drugs. I believe it is now known as CVS, after some corporate buyout. Anyway, we shopped the heck out of that Eckerd Drug. I remember going up and down those two Christmas aisles and getting all my favorite Christmas candies, especially the liquid-filled chocolate-covered cherries. Those are still my favorites. We also got ornaments, lights, tinsel, garland, and a small, white Christmas tree. That poor thing didn't last long.

We took the tree home and put it up in our little apartment. We moved the furniture away from a corner near the window and the air conditioner unit. This was before pre-lit trees and central air took over the world. My mom and I had to pull the lights from the box ever so carefully. God forbid you should break a bulb. Then, the whole damn string would not work. After we, well she, I was about 10 at this time, cursed at the tree and the lights for a bit, we plugged them in. The beautiful multicolor lights made Santa and magic seem real.

Next, we got out the silver garland. I have always liked silver better than gold, so I requested silver. We placed it all around the tree, careful not to cover or disturb the lights. I helped place the garland in the back of the tree because I could still fit in that tiny corner. I had a half-eaten candy cane hanging out of my mouth like a skinny, minty cigar.

Next came the ornaments. Pretty much all ornaments were made of glass back then. This was before everything was plastic. They were cheap Eckerd Drug ornaments, but they were still shiny and colorful. Mom and I never had fancy-themed trees. We just had multicolored everything trees. It's good that we bought the little white tree, as this provided a good background for our redgreenpinkpurplebluesilver decorations.

Once we got the ornaments on, my cat, Miss Kitty, started chasing the shiny reflections on the wall. Miss Kitty loved the Christmas tree and especially the tinsel. The strands were probably like snakes to her. This was way back in the day before we knew pet owners should not use tinsel. I'm sure Miss Kitty pooped her share of silver snaky brownness.

I'm not sure what day it was, or what the exact reason was, but my mom got really pissed off about Christmas. It was hard to tell what would set my mom off. I don't remember if there were presents under the tree or not. I don't remember if it was before or after Christmas. I just remember the colorful glass everywhere and being yelled at for crying about it. I picked up tiny, colorful shards from the shag carpet. I was glad that Miss Kitty was outside and would not accidentally be cut by the ornaments.

My mom wasn't the only one who knew how to fuck up the holiday spirit. One year, it was planned that I would actually visit my father at Christmas. His parents, my-always-absent-from-my-life grandparents, would be there. It would give them an opportunity to see me, not that they really cared that much. When I was born, my mother and father were in the middle of a divorce. So, my father thought it would be a great idea to tell everyone that I was not his child. He portrayed my mom as some wild woman who had an affair and got pregnant. Then, when I started to look JUST LIKE HIS MOM, everyone kind of knew my father was an asshole. That still didn't make the Petty family really interested in getting to know me as a person. But I'm not bitter or anything.

Since I would be going to my father's house for Christmas, he called my mother and asked her what I wanted for Christmas. He also asked her what Santa would be bringing for me at my mom's house. Then, in his never-ending attempt to screw with my mom, my father went out and bought the same presents. He literally duplicated ALL of the presents my mom had already purchased. Of course, my mom and I didn't realize this until I got to my dad's and opened them, again, there. Only I thought Santa got all the presents for me, and I was super confused as to why he would get me two of everything. I was really disappointed because I didn't get unique gifts. That was the only time I spent Christmas with my father.

1983 | Tossing Duke

Seventh grade was one of the worst years of my life. I was a short, chubby girl who wore the wrong clothes and went to a harsh middle school in a rough part of town. McNichol Middle School was hectic, to say the least. There was always a fight, and I was beaten up twice during my two-year stint. I didn't fit into any of the cliques. I wasn't tough enough to be a gangbanger. I threw up when I tried to smoke, so I couldn't be a burnout. I lacked the designer clothes, decent house, and new car required to be a preppie. Yes, there were preppies at that horrible school. So, I spent a lot of time being afraid of everything and everyone. I hated life that year.

The teachers and administrators were severe, as well. During my seventh-grade year, a new rule was created to help reduce tardiness. If students were late to class, the teacher was to send them to the office to "get a pass." Getting a pass included a spanking. In 1983, the principal could still hit you.

One day, I was called out of class to go to the guidance office. I was immediately frightened. My stomach hurt. I assumed I was in trouble, even though I really couldn't think of what I had done. Maybe they had found out about the Tylenol 3 that my mom told me to take at school for cramps. I focused on the sound of my K-Mart parachute pants rubbing together to get my mind off of my anxiety as I made my way from class to the guidance office. By the time I got to the office, which was a two-minute walk from the classroom, I was sweaty from the back of my neck to my armpits. Parachute pants, especially the black ones I wore, were not exactly the most breathable garment to wear in hot and humid South Florida.

There were three other kids in the office when I got there. The guidance counselor brought us into her office and closed the door. Holy hell! I didn't even really know these kids, but I knew they were smart and never got in trouble. I knew of them from being in the same elective classes with them, but I didn't talk to them. How could I possibly have gotten into trouble with them? I sat down on a small wooden chair that should have been in an elementary school and waited for the guidance counselor to speak to us.

She started talking about college, Duke University, to be exact. She explained that Duke University was a pretty big deal in the college world. Really, until then, I hadn't thought about college. I just wanted to make it to high school and graduate without getting pregnant like my mom did. I was sitting there wondering why she was talking to us, me and these random kids, about Duke University. Maybe they had meant to call another Lisa to the office. Surely, I was not college material.

Ms. Guidance Counselor Lady (not her name, as far as I know) told us we had been chosen to take the SAT for Duke's annual talent search. When she said SAT, I thought of the CAT (California Achievement Test) that we took every year and my stomach released its vice grip. I kind of enjoyed taking tests like that because we didn't have to do schoolwork, everyone was quiet, and we got to have a snack. Did I mention I liked to eat? She clarified the SAT wasn't the same as the CAT. We wouldn't be taking the test during school time but on the weekend at a high school. She sent us home with informational packets for our parents. Grudgingly, I handed over the packet to my mom when she got home from work that day.

My mom took the packet from my hands and gave me a warning look. This look told me that she suspected this was bad news. I remained quiet and sat on the blue loveseat we had gotten from Sears. Once my mom had a chance to look at the information in the packet, she was thrilled. She explained that if I did well on this test, I could maybe go to Duke for free. I wasn't exactly sure where Duke was, but I knew it was far away. I also knew that this test seemed important, and I wasn't sure if I was smart enough to take it.

My mom and I sat at the kitchen table in our two-bedroom duplex that night after eating Hungry Man turkey dinners, and we filled out little bubbles on the application sheet. Then, we put everything in an envelope, and Mom added it to the outgoing mail pile at work that next morning. Once Duke received the application sheet, they would send us the date and time for when I could take the test. In the meantime, I was supposed to look at the sample test and try to prepare to take the SAT in a few weeks.

I started flipping through the sample test while I sat on the floor in front of the TV, with MTV on in the background. The English part didn't seem too bad, but the math problems got blurry as I stared at them, trying to understand all of the X and Y equations. I was in my second quarter of pre-algebra at this point, a class I would end up failing. Of course, I immediately started dwelling on what would happen if I failed the test. How could anyone possibly think that I was good enough to take the SAT at 12? I wasn't smart. I wasn't good enough to have a normal family, or house, or friends, or anything. These people obviously didn't understand what a loser I was. There was no way that I could take this test. No way.

One day, after school, I walked from the bus to the front porch of the front apartment and checked our mail slowly so everyone on the bus would think I lived in a regular house with a porch and not in the apartment in back; I saw an envelope from The College Board. The pit of my stomach pinched me. I got home a couple of hours before my mom, which meant that I got the mail, and I usually just put it on the table for her to look at after work. I held the large envelope in my hand after I had put the bills and catalogs down. I knew that there was no way that I could pass this test, and when I failed it, my mom was going to be mad at me. I knew that

I couldn't take it. I took the envelope around to the back of the duplex, and I walked down the gravelly alley behind our backyard. I turned right on Fillmore Street and headed towards the small apartment building next to the pay phone I used to call people when I was grounded from using the phone at home. There was a big green open dumpster over the short cement wall. I hoisted myself up so I could sit on the hot cement, burning my hands a little. Then, I carefully got up to a standing position and tossed the envelope into the dumpster. I jumped down from the wall and landed hard in my flip-flops, hurting my feet but feeling much better overall. I was not going to take the SAT, at least not for another four years.

1983 | Codeine in the Girls' Room

I sat there in math class with my left arm wrapped around my lower abdomen, while I attempted to do a long division problem. My stomach had been hurting all morning and I thought it was my normal going-to-school stomachache. Unlike my everyday stomach pain, this one was not going away. I had just turned 11 three weeks before, and I was still playing with Barbies, so I didn't suspect that I was getting my period. I asked Creepy Bald Math Teacher (not his real name) for a pass to the bathroom.

When I got to the bathroom, I was relieved that it was empty. I suspected that I might have to do the dreaded school poop. I put toilet paper on the seat, pulled down my pink threaded Sears Pretty Plus jeans, and sat down to poop. Only as soon as I sat down, I noticed brown stuff in my underwear. I thought I had shit myself. I got up, pulled up my pants, and went to the office to call my mom. Obviously, I was sick.

The office sent a student aid to my math class to get my Jordache purse and books while I sat on a plastic chair and waited for my mom, feeling nervous because she sounded mad on the phone. Mom asked me what exact sickness I had when I got in the car, and I told her I had a stomachache, but I had not thrown up or anything. She sort of rolled her eyes but put the Sunbird in drive and exited the parking lot. On the way home, Mom decided to get some food since this time away from work would count as her lunch break. After driving through Burger King and telling me I didn't seem sick enough for her to take off work to pick me up,

Mom dropped me off at home. As soon as she left, I left my food on the table and walked up to the front apartment where my friend Melanie lived. I told her about what happened and she gave me some panty liners, and for a while, panty liners were all I needed. I didn't get my period again for months, and when I did, it was light and brown again. It wasn't until seventh grade when Mother Nature reared her really ugly head at me. This is when I started needing real maxi pads and pain relief.

Back in the early 80s, ibuprofen didn't exist, at least not in its over-the-counter sweet-coated Advil form. We had Tylenol and aspirin for cramps. Aspirin has always, even when I was a kid, and even when I take it with food, eaten my stomach. Since aspirin was a no, I tried Tylenol, which worked like a placebo. Nothing worked for my cramps.

One day, I asked my mom if I could stay home from school and use the heating pad because I had cramps. My mom almost never let me miss school. I had to be vomiting or have a fever in order to stay home in the morning. She told me I would have cramps my whole life and should get used to them, but she did have something that would help with the pain. Mom went into her room and came back with a small bottle of red liquid.

"Here! Take a couple of sips of this." She handed the bottle to me.

I pushed down on the cap and turned it at the same time to open it. Then, I did as I was told. The red liquid tasted kind of sweet, not too bad. I looked at the bottle and saw "Tylenol No. 3." I sort of rolled my eyes, as I already knew that Tylenol did not work, and said, "What is this?"

My mom answered, "It's Tylenol No. 3. I got it from work. Just put it in your purse and go into the bathroom stall at lunch and take a couple more sips. You'll be fine." By "got it from work," Mom meant she stole it from the sample closet at the doctor's office where she was a secretary. I figured if they had it in the supply closet and it had a three in the name, it must be some sort of super Tylenol. Maybe it would work.

And work it did. It took away my cramps and some of my anxiety about going to McNichol. At lunchtime, I snuck into the bathroom and took another couple of gulps. I had no idea I was taking narcotics at school. I tucked the small bottle of red liquid into my yellow Jordache purse along with my 1980s boat-sized maxi pads, without wings, every morning during my period and went to school.

I wish I had a great story about being caught with codeine in school and being arrested, but I don't. I successfully entered the bathroom stall a couple of times a day and took two swigs of Tylenol 3 whenever I changed my pad. That stuff really worked. I still can't believe I got away with basically doing drugs at school, even though I wasn't aware I was doing "drugs." I thought it was just Tylenol. Maybe that is why no one suspected. I was that innocent kid that most teachers liked. MOST.

My seventh-grade English teacher was not a fan. I think this had something to do with my never participating in discussions and waiting until the last minute to do any writing assignment, which meant I turned in a sloppy, handwritten crappy essay each time. It is really no surprise that she is the reason I got paddled at school for coming back from the bathroom late during one of the pad and codeine visits.

I had English right after lunch, so she NEVER let anyone use the bathroom. She told us we had plenty of time to go during lunch. One day, when I had cramps, I went on my way from lunch to English. Unfortunately, given the diaper change I had to do, I was one minute late to class. When I got to the classroom, the door was locked. I did what any sane person would do. I knocked. She opened the door and told me to go to the office to "get a pass." Fuck.

I walked to the office like I was on my way to the lethal injection room in prison. I carried my books in the crook of my left arm and my yellow Jordache purse containing a class three controlled substance over my right shoulder. When I got to the front office, I walked up to the tall brown desk, and I politely asked for a pass.

The lady behind the desk asked me why I was late, and I explained that I had to use the restroom before class. She said I would need to see the assistant principal for a pass. Fuck again.

I sat in one of the plastic chairs, waiting for him to call me in. He asked me why I was late, and I repeated what I had told the secretary, that I simply had to use the bathroom. He asked me why I hadn't gone during lunch and I said, "I don't know."

He shook his head and laughed, saying something about him hoping I remember this for next time. I thought we were done, and turned to walk out of his office.

"Oh no! Where are you going? We're not done," he said, and I turned back around, knowing what was about to happen. He seemed happy to grab that paddle. He told me they were cracking down on kids skipping class. I kept quiet because I feared men, and I was embarrassed about having my period. Given the sexual abuse and watching my mom get beaten by her boyfriend, this was understandable. Even though I was not skipping class, and I was only one minute late to class, the assistant principal told me I would be spanked. My mother had signed the corporal punishment permission form, so he was all good to hit me.

He had me bend over his desk, and he gave me only one whack, but it was a good one. I got tears in my eyes when that paddle hit my Gloria Vanderbilt black denim jeans that I had just gotten for Christmas that year. I didn't let myself cry, though. After he hit me, he put the paddle down on his desk and handed me a pass to class. I took the piece of pink paper and walked out of the office. It was a horrible experience, but at least he didn't search my purse. I can only imagine what my punishment would be for "skipping" and having narcotics in my purse.

1984 : The Great Escape

I was a little nervous on the morning of my first day at Olsen Middle, but I was glad to be changing schools. The previous year, the school board had voted to change the school boundaries. So, instead of going back to McNichol for eighth grade, I could finally go to Olsen, the school I was supposed to be going to anyway, if my mom had used our real address instead of using the Mitchells' information.

My mom dropped me off at the bus stop, which was a block away from the Atrium Apartments, where we had moved the previous November after leaving the duplex on 24th Avenue. The Atrium was a larger building with two floors, and it was nicer. I was so happy to be living in a better apartment, even if it wasn't a normal house. And now I was going to a better school. If only Rod were totally out of the picture, life would be pretty good.

I didn't know anyone at the bus stop, so I just stood there quietly on the weed-ridden cracked sidewalk in my Valente Jeans and large Ocean Pacific T-shirt. As I looked around, I noticed a couple of younger kids, sixth graders, and then there was a girl about my age who ended up being in seventh grade. Her name was (and still is) Hillary and she changed my life.

Hillary said hello and asked me my name. After introducing myself, we started chatting about middle school girl things like clothes and Wham. Since I was nervous, I started cracking jokes. That is still what I do when I don't know what else to say. I make a stupid joke about something. Well, I was in luck, because Hillary appreciated jokes. We ended up sitting on the bus together and cracking all kinds of jokes.

Since Hillary was in seventh grade, we didn't have any classes together. So, I said bye to her when we got to school and went off to the eighth-grade hall to find my first class. I don't remember what I had first period, but I remember what I had right before lunch—math. Since I had failed it in seventh grade, which was the only class I had ever failed, I had to take pre-algebra in eighth grade. Again. I knew no one.

I walked in and sat in the row closest to the chalkboard. I squinted up at the board, which had some formulas on it and the proper way to put a heading on our papers. I took out my green math folder from my Trapper Keeper and put it on my desk. As I was about to get out some notebook paper, I noticed that the tape I had put on the front of the folder to repair a small tear was curling up. So, I used one of my long fingernails and started rubbing the tape back into place. I kind of started daydreaming and kept rubbing the tape longer than necessary.

"That looks like fun," the girl sitting behind me said. I turned around to see a cute blonde girl with glasses. I would later learn that her name was Marilyn.

"Oh yeah. I do this at all my parties," I answered, joking because I had no idea what to say. I had never hosted a party, and even if I had, I doubted I would pull out the tape and ripped folders as entertainment.

Marilyn laughed out loud and told her friends what I had said. They thought it was mildly amusing and gave a little chuckle. Marilyn invited me to sit with them at lunch after class.

I met more of her friends at lunch. I found out they knew Hillary, too and she sat with us because she had the same lunch period we did. I was so happy to be sitting with nice people who did not smell like cigarette smoke. Right then, I realized McNichol Lisa was dead. Olsen Lisa was sitting with the cool kids. It was the best first day of school I had ever had.

I may have had popular friends, but I was still a new kid, and new kids got picked on. One day, I was walking with my friends back to class after lunch, and I heard "PIG LIPS!!" I ignored it, not thinking it was directed at me.

"HEY! PIG LIPS!!" I ignored it again and walked into my class.

It didn't stop. Finally, the person yelling "PIG LIPS" made it clear that I was Pig Lips. That was my new name because I had giant lips. I knew my lips were too big to play the flute and all, but I never thought they were big enough to be referred to as pig lips. And I wondered if pigs really had big lips anyway.

I was so embarrassed whenever this group of jerks would start yelling pig lips at me. I cried at home many times. Then, I got angry and started to fight back. My first step was to get one of the offender's phone numbers. My friend and I prank-called him. Then, after my mom started dating John, he called him and threatened to break his legs. For real. That is just how some old-school Italian World War II veterans roll.

Since John wasn't going to break anyone's legs, and since I had to deal with this situation somehow, I thought up my own names for two of the guys. One guy had bright blue eyes, but his eyelids were noticeably brown. So, I called him Liver Lids. Yes, that is totally creative, I know. The other one had a nose that Toucan Sam would envy. He became Hose Nose. My insults and John's threats did not stop them from harassing me at school and other places.

One Friday evening, I went to the movies with my friends Theresa and Marilyn, along with a few others. It was about 7:00 pm and we had just stepped into the lobby when I heard it.

"PIGLIPS!!"

It was those idiots from school. Theresa and Marilyn told me to ignore them as we got our sodas and popcorn. We made it into the theater to see *Ladyhawke* without a confrontation, though I was mad enough to hit them if I had run into them.

As we were sitting there, chatting before the previews started, the whole asshole crew walked in: Hose Nose, Liver lids, and some dude named Greg who was not interesting enough to have a nickname. He actually was an okay guy when he was not hanging with these idiots.

My anger built as the movie went on, and I stared at the backs of their heads. I barely paid attention to Matthew Broderick and Michelle Pfeiffer, who was the titular character. One character was a scruffy old man with hair like a used Brillo pad. Whenever he appeared on screen, I yelled, "There's Jon's mom!" Jon was Hose Nose's name in the world outside of our feud.

As soon as we exited the theater, they started making fun of me again. We had thrown our trash away on the way out, but I still had my large Coke. All it took was two rounds of "PIGLIPS!" to make me angry and frustrated.

"Stop calling me that!" I said, or at least I think I did. I might have said, "Screw off, Jon!" or something like that. All I know for sure is that I threw that large Coke right at him, and I had good aim. It landed all over his shirt. Everyone laughed, even me and Jon. It seemed to have broken the tension between us, and they stopped calling me "Pig Lips."

About a month or so after that, after hanging out all day during the eighth-grade trip to Disney World, Jon and I started dating. That's teenagers for you! We saw each other all through the summer, seeing *Back to the Future* numerous times without really watching it until we broke up a couple of weeks after beginning high school at different schools. I still have my eighth-grade yearbook with Jon's long, kind message that ended with, "P.S. Drink Sprite; it doesn't stain." I drink Diet Coke now, but I haven't thrown it at anyone.

Around this same time, Burdines, a fancy department store in South Florida, started offering modeling classes for girls. I wanted to model, even though I was super short with huge lips. I convinced some of my new friends to take the class with me. We ended up with a crew of about five. Marilyn, the one who laughed at my tape joke on the first day, was one of them. Cathy, Amy, Theresa, and Kim also joined us.

The Burdines' modeling classes were taught by a woman who probably did most of her modeling in the sixties. We learned how to use Dippity Doo hair gel and hot rollers. We also learned about the fine art of using cold cream to remove makeup. We learned how to walk and pivot on a runway. We even starred in a fashion show in the Burdines junior department. But that wasn't my favorite part of modeling classes.

The best part about modeling was hanging out with my friends in the mall after class. We thought we were super cool eighth graders strutting through the Hollywood Fashion Center. We browsed the jeans in Renegade like we owned the place. We went to Sbarro for pizza without any grown-ups. We even sat at the counter, right by the griddle and ovens. One time, while we were chattering away, one of Cathy's rubber bands from her braces popped off and landed on the griddle. We all laughed until we thought we would pee ourselves. We did not tell the waitress, though. Oops.

It was great to have friends and to be allowed to go out with them. Until eighth grade, my mom had been very protective. Once she realized I was hanging out with people who did not smoke or skip class, she eased up a little. She even let me go to the movies at night without her.

The Sheridan Seven was the happening place to be in 1985. It was the nicest movie theater I had ever been to, and it had SEVEN theaters. This was unheard of. Usually, our theaters could only show two movies at a time. SEVEN was amazing. Not only did we hang out in the theater, but we sat around on curbs and cement parking blocks for hours after the movie. If we got hungry, we walked over to Burger King and got a bunch of kid meals.

Going to Olsen and meeting Hillary and the rest of my new friends changed my life for the better. During my eighth-grade year, I had more fun and did better in my classes than I had at

McNichol. My mom met and became engaged to my stepdad that year, too. I was hoping they would buy a real house after they got married, and we could finally, FINALLY, be normal.

    Nope.

1984 : Convenience Store Surprise Party

I didn't get the idea until I was on the bus on the way home from school. Well, really, I didn't get the idea at all; it was Hillary's idea. I had told Hillary how my mom was often angry after work and how she would scream at me for any little thing, like the apartment not being perfectly clean. Hillary had witnessed a couple of my mom's tirades, too, so she knew why I was anxious about my mom's birthday. I was really worried that my mom would be extra angry on her 40th birthday. From what I saw on TV and in the movies, turning forty was something really sad. I was so anxious about going home that I had a stomachache. That's when Hillary came up with the brilliant idea.

"You should throw her a surprise party," Hillary said to me, turning sideways in her seat so that we were facing each other. We were sitting across the aisle from each other, with our backs against the bus windows and our legs stretched out.

"Yeah, right! She'd probably get mad at me for getting streamers on the floor. Plus, her birthday is TODAY. I don't have time to plan a party or any money." I rolled my eyes.

Hillary got this look on her face like she had the best idea ever. "I can get my mom to help, and we can get stuff at Dunham's!"

Dunham's was a small convenience store next to our bus stop. It was a true mom-and-pop store, and it was tiny, probably 700 square feet at most, with creaky hardwood floors and a very limited selection of food. Hillary and I went there just about every day to get ice cream or a candy bar. So, we knew we could at least get a couple of bags of chips and a bottle of Diet Coke, my mom's favorite.

As soon as we got off the bus, we ran through people's yards to Hillary's house to tell her mom what we wanted to do. She gave us a little money, and then we scraped together a few more bucks between Hillary's Esprit and my Jordache purses. We had just enough to get a bag of Ruffles, some sour cream and onion dip in a can, and a two-liter of Diet Coke.

We lugged our bags to my apartment building and up the stairs. We put the Diet Coke in the fridge immediately because warm soda really annoyed my mom. Hillary and I tried to decorate the living room by making our own birthday signs with paper and markers. I called Fran to see if she and Nicole, who was six at this time, could come over before my mom got home. Hillary's mom and sister Megan came over, too.

My mom wasn't a big fan of Hillary's mom because she had once told Hillary that she could never sleep over at my house because my mom was a "divorcee." At least, that is what my mom told me. I guess back in 1984, being a "divorcee" meant you held swinger parties and gave drugs to children. Anyway, Hillary never slept over at my house.

So, even though it was last minute, and Fran was not a last-minute kind of person, she made it and she brought a small cake. Hillary and I filled the little apartment's living room with Fran and Nicole, Hillary's mom and little sister, Hillary, and me.

We all yelled "SURPRISE!" when she walked in the door. Mom was surprised, all right. Later, after she sat down on the loveseat with a cup of Diet Coke and some chips and dip, she asked me why I threw a party for her, and I told her the truth. I was afraid she would be mad about turning 40. She thought it was silly that I would be afraid that she would be upset about her 40th birthday. She did that thing where she acted like she didn't have a Mommy

Dearest temper. She chuckled over her silly daughter being worried about her being pissed off. Everyone chuckled with her except Hillary and me. We knew.

1984 | Halloween Assholes

My mom was super angry one particular Saturday morning in October. We were out running our usual errands, grocery shopping at Pantry Pride, and dropping off the laundry at the place on Dixie Highway, and out of nowhere, something had made her mad. She screeched to a stop at all the red lights and stop signs, bending her knee a bit to slam on the brakes. Since she was 4' 11", she didn't have to bend it much, but she gave it her all. I sat in the passenger seat of the Pontiac Sunbird, holding onto the door handle with my right hand and my seatbelt with the left. Not everyone had to wear seatbelts in Florida in 1984, but I did, especially when my mom was in a wicked-witch mood.

I was trying to think of a way to get her back to being in a good mood. I figured maybe I could get her talking about something silly. Halloween was a few weeks away, so I asked, "Mom, what are you going to be for Halloween?" after we had screeched to a stop at the traffic light two blocks from home.

Mom wasn't having it. "A FUCKING ASSHOLE!" she yelled at me.

I figured that was my cue to shut up. When we got home, we each went to our rooms after carrying the groceries upstairs and putting them away. My mom slammed her door, but I left mine open so I could hear her. She had tried to overdose twice by this time, and I always got nervous when she was angry and went into her room like that. From what I could tell, she was only changing clothes. I didn't hear any pill bottles rattling, so I figured this was a normal tantrum, not a super scary one.

She came out of her room about twenty minutes later and sat on the couch to read *The Enquirer*. I waited until after I had heard her turn a few pages, then I put my key in my shorts pocket and walked to the living room. "Um, Mom, can I go to Hillary's for a little bit?" I looked down at my white Keds and waited for a response.

Mom sat there in her terry cloth jumper that she wore around the house, the one with the little flecks of nail polish on it because she wore it every Sunday when she did her nails. She looked up from The Enquirer and said, "Okay. Just be home by four to help me pick up the laundry and dinner." Dinner on Saturdays was usually Kentucky Fried Chicken. That's what they called it before everything became an acronym. Mom seemed calm, not quite happy, but not angry like she had been earlier. I took this as a good sign and headed to Hillary's.

I was so grateful that my best friend's house was close by. It was only two blocks if you stuck to the sidewalk, but we had a shortcut. From my apartment building, the larger Atrium, I crossed the street and walked between the smaller Atrium apartment building and the house where the foster kids lived. Then, I walked past the run-down townhouses and the duplexes to the next street, Taylor Street. Once I crossed Taylor Street, I was almost in Hillary's backyard. If there wasn't a fence, I probably could have walked in the back door, but I went around to the front and saw her brothers, Josh and Justin, sitting on the front stoop.

They told me Hillary was in her room and to go on in. I was there a lot that year. They were used to seeing me stomp up the brick steps. I opened the door and stepped in, stopping while her Rottweiler sniffed me. He had finally gotten used to me and no longer charged at me. I walked around the corner to Hillary's room. She was sitting on her bed, reading, when I walked in. As soon as she saw my face, she knew something was off.

"What's wrong?" Hillary put a bookmark in her book and set it down.

"UGH. My mom is all mad about something again." I sat down at the edge of her bed, close to tears but relieved to be away from my mom.

"AWW!" Hillary patted my arm. She had witnessed my mom's temper a couple of times.

"Yep, and I tried to cheer her up by asking her what she wanted to be for Halloween, and she yelled at me and said "a fucking asshole!'" I kicked off my Keds and curled up on Hillary's bed.

Hillary fell back next to me and laughed. "Really? That's what she said?" She laughed some more.

I was confused. How was she laughing at this? "Yes. She yelled it at me. Why are you laughing?"

Hillary sat back up and looked at me. "Lisa, just imagine this costume!"

I looked over at her. I was still confused. "An asshole costume?"

Hillary said, laughing, "Yes! We could be assholes for Halloween, too! We could get brown lipstick and some brown fuzzy sweaters."

I pictured our asshole costumes then. "OH! And we could chew up some chocolate and spit a little out when we say, "Trick or treat!" I added.

Hillary kept going with it. "YES! And we could cut up Brillo pads and glue the pieces to our faces, like pubes!"

We both rolled around on Hillary's twin bed, laughing and adding to our costumes until her four-year-old sister Megan came in, and we had to stop talking about assholes. I felt much better after having a good laugh with Hillary. We never made those asshole costumes, but I think back to us designing them every Halloween. Hillary was a good friend to me that year, one of the best friends I ever had. She even witnessed my first panic attack.

I remember feeling like something bad was going to happen when Hillary's mom dropped us off at Six Flags Atlantis. Hillary and I were 13, and we were there for an outdoor concert by Cheap Trick, a band we didn't really know that was making a comeback in the mid-80s.

Hillary and I were thrilled to be there. We splashed our way down the water walkway, or water sidewalk, or whatever the official name was. It was much needed as the pavement in the park was at least a thousand degrees and everyone was running around barefoot. We weren't allowed to get on the slides with our shoes on.

We got to the concert site, behind a pair of water slides at the back of the park, early. So, since this was our first concert, we did the super smart thing and stood RIGHT IN FRONT of the stage. I mean, like we were touching the stage. Neither one of us thought about the fact that other people, and lots of them, would be there soon, and those people might try to get close to the stage, too.

Soon, those other people arrived and crowded around us. When Cheap Trick started playing, EVERYONE pushed forward. I felt like I couldn't breathe. I turned to the side and yelled at a woman next to me to LET ME OUT! She tried, but no one would move. My heart was racing. I felt like I could puke. There was no way I could get out.

Until Jimmy passed out. I didn't know him. It was the summer before I started high school, and he was a year older. I knew he was cute and unconscious. People were carrying him out of the crowd. I joined them. This was my ticket out. I told Jimmy about this years later, and he insists his fainting was not drug-related.

After that concert, I realized I didn't like being in the center of crowds. I also realized that I didn't really like concerts all that much. I figured as long as I stayed away from those types of situations, that I would never feel panic like I did that day. I was wrong.

1984 | As Foretold by Astrology: An Old Man and a Pool

My mom and I were checking our mail at the Atrium apartments on City Hall Circle after a day at the Broward County Fair. I was holding a small mirror with a Def Leppard logo on it and still savoring the fried dough I had devoured at the fair. It was our tradition to go to the fair on Black Friday rather than go shopping like the rest of the world. It was more fun and more affordable.

My mom had her key in the small metal mailbox, and she was sorting through the latest delivery of bills when this tall, bald, old man started talking to her. He was loud. I don't remember exactly what he said because I was 13 and really did not care what he was saying. Also, I didn't want to be too friendly because my mom tended to develop relationships with scary men. Plus, I didn't think I had to get to know this one. He looked like someone's grandpa. I soon learned he wasn't anyone's grandpa, and his name was John.

I had seen him around. When John first moved to the Atrium, he was in apartment 101, right next door to Geneva, our hairdresser who had told us about the Atrium. Geneva and Frankie, her partner, would hear John yelling at one of his sons who visited him from Boston, where John was from. One time, when we were visiting Geneva, we went into her kitchen and listened to the yelling with her as it was happening on the other side of that wall. It was a lot more interesting than pretending to eat the microwaved chicken breast and onions she had made for dinner.

Before we met John, or even knew of his booming voice, my mom had learned that the love of her life was coming and she would meet him "near water." That's what the astrologer told my mom when she did her chart and talked her through it. My mom recorded it on an old tape recorder and let me listen to the tape. I rolled my eyes at "near water." We lived in Florida, for fuck's sake. I didn't say "for fuck's sake" aloud as my mom would have smacked the living shit out of me even though she spoke like a "long shahman" as John would say, once they got to know each other.

So, there we were meeting him near water. At the time, it didn't dawn on me that THIS was the love of her life who would help usher her into the period that the astrologer referred to as "your time, baby." I was tired from our day at the fair and I just wanted to go upstairs and watch TV.

John invited my mom to dinner a couple of days after meeting her by saying, "I don't wanna eat alone. My wife just died a couple of months ago." The man had game, and he really was newly widowed. She went to dinner with him. After a few dates, they decided it was time for me to walk downstairs with Mom to eat dinner at John's apartment, which was 104 now. He didn't like 101 as it was at the end of the building, and EVERYONE walked by. It was noisy.

John made some sort of pasta. He was Italian and this was back when carbs were good and fat was bad. I loved pasta, still do, so I sat there and inhaled dinner, while stopping to make cracks about John's bald head, or his age, or his nose. I was 13 and I had lived through my mom's previous relationships. I was trying to send John running.

No such luck. John didn't get angry when I insulted him. He laughed. He said, "You got the gift of gab kid! You remind me of Joan Rivers."

I crinkled my nose. "Who is Joan Rivers?"

He was shocked. "You don't know Joan Rivers?! Madonna mi! She's a comedian."

Guess what he got me for Christmas that first year? A Joan River's album. I fell in love with her instantly, and I started watching other comedians on TV late at night. Ten years later, I began performing stand-up comedy myself. I now know that he inspired me. He saw my talent and the real me.

But when I was 13, he was annoying and embarrassing. A few months after my mom started dating John, she brought him to my school, Olsen Middle, to watch me MC the spring talent show. When the show ended, I was chatting with friends, when a boy yelled to me that my "grandpa" was looking for me. I felt my face turn red as I ran out of the backstage area and down the steps to see John and my mom waiting for me. "Come on, kid! Let's go!"

And go we did. We walked to the parking lot to his super uncool ten-year-old green Lincoln Town Car. Three years later, I would learn how to drive in that beast of a car. I still hated it.

John didn't just teach me how to drive; he taught me how to eat.

Like a lot of low-income families, Mom and I didn't exactly eat healthy food. We were on food stamps back when they looked like Monopoly money and not those discreet little cards. We did get an enormous block of American cheese for free a few times, too. Don't knock it. The government cheese is delicious. It makes great sandwiches and awesome mac and cheese.

"Yah a shit eatah, Jan!" That is exactly what John said to my mom every time she suggested using a canned or jarred item instead of making it from scratch.

He wasn't wrong. My mom and I had been shit-eaters for 13 years before she met John. Some of my happiest childhood memories involve eating "bad" food, and I'm not just talking tater tot day in elementary school. My mom and I graced the drive-throughs of Hollywood, Florida every Saturday and Sunday evening, and sometimes more often.

Every Saturday morning, we would wake up and get dressed right away. My mom would carry our laundry basket to the rusted green Chevy that was one floor hole short of being a Flintstone mobile. The laundry would be in the back seat, and I would be in the front seat. We were off to drop off our laundry at City-Wide Fabric Care on Washington and Dixie in lovely Hollywood, Florida. My mom made very little money from her job as a receptionist at Children's Medical Center, but she'd be damned if she would spend her time off doing laundry, especially since she would need to sit in a laundromat to do it. Our rental duplex on Taylor Street and Dixie Highway did not come with a washer and dryer.

After we dropped off the laundry, it was breakfast time. We didn't go to McDonalds or back home for some cereal. No. We went out for a proper hot breakfast every weekend day. WAGS was a favorite of ours. They had the best strawberry French toast. We also enjoyed Kith and Kin, one of the first quirky southern joints to serve beverages in jars. That is where I learned to love grits.

With our bellies full, sometimes too full, we were on our way to our next task — grocery shopping at Pantry Pride. We didn't learn about the heaven that is Publix until my mom married my stepdad. He always shopped at Publix. Anyway, while we were at Pantry Pride, we would always buy frozen meals for dinner during the week. Sometimes, we could get FANCY frozen meals that included things like beef burgundy or chicken divan.

By the time we put the groceries away and did the weekly vacuuming and dusting, it was time to pick up the laundry. Mom drove us back over to City-Wide, and we both went in to get the laundry. My mom's work clothes, mostly polyester pants and blouses, were on hangers and in plastic. I carried them to the car and hung them as best as I could from the tiny, green plastic hook in the back seat. Mom picked up the basket with fresh, folded clothes and towels inside and "Patty" written in sharpy on the outside of the basket. Our last name was Petty, and my mom's first name was Janet, but the laundry lady always called her Patty.

Our Saturday routine always ended with KFC. We always got two-piece dark meals with two mashed potatoes and no coleslaw. Back then, the only sides KFC had were coleslaw, mashed potatoes, and corn on the cob. They also had dinner rolls instead of biscuits. Scary times!

With the laundry safely in the back seat, I sat up front and performed my official duty as food protector. I had to hold on to both KFC meal boxes so they would not go flying if mom hit the brakes too hard. I'm pretty sure we did not wear seat belts back then, so I'm not sure how I didn't go flying.

On some weekends, my teen brother would come for a visit. Our father still had custody of him, and mom had me. Mom would have to drive to Miami on Friday nights to pick him up and then drop him off on Sunday evenings. My dad was a giant dick to my mom and refused to help with transportation. By the time we got back to Hollywood from dropping my brother off in Miami, Mom didn't feel like cooking dinner at all, not even putting a fancy Le Menu or normal Swanson in the oven. So, a lot of times, we would drive through Burger King on the way home. It was usually quick and allowed us to get home and eat our cheeseburgers while watching Sonny and Cher.

Except for that one Sunday. The guy in the car in front of us was waiting FOREVER at the window for his food. My mom was getting impatient and doing those big sighs she would do when she was pissed. She was saying things to me like, "What did he order, a side of beef?" I shrugged and kept quiet lest I say something to add to her foul mood. She ended up turning off the car to save gas, and that's when it got really quiet.

Until the gentleman behind us spoke up. Just when the guy in front of us finally got his BAGS of food, he leaned out his car window and asked for ketchup. The man in the car behind us was not having it. He, too, had been waiting a long time for the man in front of us to get an order that he should have gone inside for. The man behind us leaned half of his body out of his car window and yelled, "GETCHO ketchup home MOTHER FUCK!"

As all yelling did, it scared the crap out of me. My mom started laughing so hard that she could barely see to move the car forward after Mr. Ketchup finally pulled away. She laughed when we got our food and laughed all the way home. That scary memory has stuck with me for over 40 years. Now, whenever I go through a drive-through, I decline the offer of ketchup, telling them I have plenty at home.

1986 : Losing my Father for Good

The last time I talked to my father was horrible. I was 14, and my mother had just married my stepfather. I was talking to my father on the phone at the small table in the kitchen. He had had a couple of heart attacks by then and was telling me about eating a lower-fat diet. My stepdad, who was older and had had bypass surgery, already had us on a low-fat diet. Our apartment's freezer was filled with soy meats of all kinds. I had already learned a lot about low-fat and low-cholesterol eating. I told my father this on the phone.

I also told him I was excited because my stepfather was going to adopt me, and then I would have the same last name as him and my mom. We were going to be like a "normal" family. Growing up as the lone custodial child of a single mom, I was always chasing "normal." I was THRILLED that my stepfather was going to adopt me. I told my father the good news, and he got angry and said, "Well, then, you're not my daughter anymore."

I had never really felt like his daughter. I never saw him. Years earlier, when I was in fourth grade, my dad explained to Fran why he spent so little time with me. It was on one of his rare sentimental days. He had driven to Fran's house when I wasn't there and asked to see my artwork from school because Fran kept EVERYTHING. As she was showing him a purple glittery paper mâché Easter egg I had made at St. Mark's, he teared up a bit. Fran was not having it. She told him he should spend more time with me.

He held up his hand and pointed to his pinky finger. "See this little finger?" he asked Fran. "If it were chopped off, I would miss it, but if it had never been there to begin with, I wouldn't miss it."

Basically, if he just had little to do with me, he wouldn't miss me. This explains why I saw my dad fewer than ten times from birth to age 15 when he died.

While I didn't see him a lot, and I do have memories of waiting out front for him and having him not show, the visits we had were memorable. One time, he took me to see *War Games* in the actual theater. Yes, I am that old. I remember Matthew Broderick before he looked like he could collect Social Security. I remember on our way to the theater, my father had the radio on and "Waiting on a Friend" by the Rolling Stones came on. I told my dad of my hatred for Mick Jagger. I still don't like the man. My only reason at the time was that he was ugly. Now that I am older, I hate his voice, too.

When my dad got his little green MG, he picked me up and took me to the mall. I think I was in seventh grade. This was a rough year for me as I was still going to McNichol Middle, where I had been beaten up twice and was made fun of constantly for being poor and having the wrong clothes. So, my dad bought me a pair of dark blue Jordache jeans. I got the tightest pair I could because, at 12, loose was ugly. I was in heaven! I wore them every day until some asshole at school called me on it.

One time, my dad took me out for Chinese food. It was this little takeout or eat-in place in Miami near his apartment. This was shortly after his divorce from his second wife, the woman he was dating when my mom was eight months pregnant with me. I remember him asking me about playing the clarinet. I was in the McNichol Middle Intermediate band. I didn't think it was a big deal. My dad was impressed, or at least he pretended to be. He told me the Pettys were creative and musical people. He also told me I was very intelligent. It felt like a real father-daughter relationship for that short amount of time we sat there eating fried rice.

My mom told me that a few days after that final call with my father, he called her and said he would only sign adoption papers if my mom signed something forfeiting all the child support he owed her. He owed her A LOT of child support. This angered my mother because she saw it as him selling me. She called her lawyer and told her to go after my father for back child support instead of proceeding with the adoption.

We never got the child support because my father was found dead in his car in a Denny's parking lot. It was determined that he had another heart attack, his third. The Denny's was located right off of I-95, so my father was probably driving, started to have chest pain, and pulled off into the parking lot to call for help. I never talked to my dad again. He died of a heart attack that night in an ambulance.

1986 | The Dad Realization

I got out of the "my father died" funk when I realized he really wasn't ever a father to me. Now, my stepfather, on the other hand, was a father to me. Not only did he teach me how to cook, clean, and not be an asshole, the man taught me he had my back right from the beginning.

Like a lot of people in the 80s, my stepdad KNEW that fat and cholesterol were the real enemies. As a triple bypass survivor, John introduced us to Morning Star products, skim milk, and Egg Beaters. Besides avoiding all things fat and cholesterol, he would ride his bike to the beach and down the broad walk (Hollywood Beach does **not** have a boardwalk; it's a broad walk) and back again daily. No helmet. No padded shorts. No sunscreen. Just cargo shorts, a ball cap, and his old man clip-on sunglasses. John ended up needing a knee replacement, but he lived to be 75, which was considered a good lifespan back in the day.

Before my mom even married John, he was there for me. Since he was 19 years older than my mom and already retired, he took me to the orthodontist and other appointments when Mom was working. During these drives in his HUGE green Lincoln Town Car, we had some good talks. One time, I told him about the boys at school who were calling me "pig lips." I never really thought much about my lips one way or another, but once these idiots pointed out that my lips took up half my face, I spent most of the time trying to pucker inward and hide the majority of my huge lips. John set me straight.

One day, he sat me down on the couch and put a pile of fashion magazines on the coffee table. He flipped through them and said, "Look at these girls. They get shots in their lips to make them fuller," he informed me.

"Well, they're stupid!" I said with all the seriousness an embarrassed 13-year-old girl can muster.

He didn't stop. He kept flipping through the magazines, pointing out the "gills" with full mouths, and telling me I had what women paid plastic surgeons to get. It took me years to believe him. Now that I'm in my 50s, I'm glad for my pig lips because they look a lot less pruny than skinny lips.

One of the best things my stepdad ever did was teach me how to drink. He had a very liberal policy on alcohol. He figured if you don't make it a "big no-no," then kids wouldn't want it so much. I think he's right about that. My stepdad bought me my first drink at one of those private clubs in Boston (I don't remember if it was the Elks, the Eagles, or what, but you know what I mean). I was 15, and he had just picked me up from the airport. I had flown up to meet him in Boston, where he was visiting family. My mom was going to fly up in a few days. On the way home from the airport, he had to stop by this lodge of sorts and talk to a friend. My guess is it had something to do with betting on something as the man's biggest vice was gambling. We sat down at the bar to wait for his friend, and my stepdad asked me what I wanted to drink.

"A screwdriver," I said, being sarcastic and not really knowing what the hell a screwdriver was.

He ordered it for me, and the bartender actually gave it to me. I drank it. Now, this was not the first time I ever drank alcohol. It was the 80s, and there were these things called wine coolers that high school kids could somehow get from stores. I've got lots of stories about wine coolers and the shenanigans they caused.

After that, my dad let me have drinks here and there. On New Year's Day, when I was 17, I came home from a sleepover with my friends. I told my parents about how one of my friends had drunk too much and barfed. I had no alcohol at all, so I held her hair. My dad immediately went into a lecture on "how to drink." Here are his rules:

- Stay away from the "dahk" stuff. (Dark stuff — Whiskey, dark rum, etc.)
- Stay away from the sweet stuff. (No frou-frou drinks)
- Don't Mix. (That one is pretty self-explanatory. Stick with the same drink.)
- Pace yourself. "Just keep a little buzz." (Don't overdo it.)
- Have some "water." (Stay hydrated.)

The man was right. I got all the way through college and young adulthood without barfing from drinking. I was 31 the first time I puked from alcohol, and that was the first of only three times. The three times that I have gotten sick from booze have been because I broke one or more of the drinking rules.

While John did teach me some useful things, he also shared his many bigoted thoughts with me. He told me it's called gravy, not sauce. "Only those Southern Italian greaseballs call it sauce." People from "New Yahk" were also greaseballs, in his mind. As I got to know him, I learned that there were issues with most people, except northern Italians.

John thought "Jews were the worst people in the world" because they "want all the money." And this is a man who spent his late teens fighting Nazis in World War II. Also, "the Blacks would step over their mother's body for a buck." There is no way to state it otherwise; he was a bigot. He reminded me of Archie Bunker in *All in the Family*.

Like Archie Bunker, he was a big old softie with his family. Before he came into our lives, my mom hit me regularly. She did not know how to parent without using fear. Her mother was worse, from what my mom told me. Anyway, the hitting ended when she married John.

I learned this one evening when my mom and I were arguing over whether I could have a boyfriend come over. I was 14, and this boy was 16. He had a car, so that made me instantly forget that he was a giant doofus. My mom insisted I was not allowed to date until I was 16. I knew she was worried about me dating because she had become pregnant with my brother at 16. I don't remember what I said exactly, but she was on top of me and hitting me wherever she could land a punch. John grabbed her by the shoulders, and at the same time, I pushed my feet into her abdomen. She was off of me. "STOP HITTING ME!" I yelled.

"She's a good kid, Jan," John said.

Knowing my mom, she probably told us both to fuck off. She didn't hit me for a few years after that. When she hit me again, after finding my birth control pills, that situation also involved a boy but included a snide comment about her teen pregnancy with my brother.

John's time in the military and his upbringing had made him a neat freak. He was Marie Kondo before Marie Kondo. He never saw the need for knick-knacks or collectibles. He was always throwing things away. One time, he threw out my mom's antique stove knick-knacks.

She was super pissed when she got home from work and saw the empty space on the six-level knick-knack shelves. "JOHN! Where are my stoves?"

"What?" John yelled from the kitchen, where he was making dinner.

"My black stoves! They were right here next to my Joan Rivers QVC eggs!" She yelled towards the kitchen while walking the eight steps it would take to get there in the tiny apartment.

John stepped out of the kitchen, smiling, and stood near the dining table. "Oh, those! I trew them out!"

My mom did not like that answer. "WHY? They are antiques!" She was turning red with anger.

"They're old! What are you gonna do with 'em?" That was his catchphrase. He said that all the time, especially while opening presents. "Take this back! What am I gonna do with it?" He applied that logic to my mom's possessions, though, and it didn't work.

My mom ordered him to walk down to the dumpster and get her stoves back. "Jan, they remind me of the depression! Seriously, what are you gonna do with 'em?" Mom did not answer that. She walked into their bedroom and slammed the door.

John looked at me and asked, "Why does she like all this tchotchke stuff?" I shrugged. I had to agree with him on this one. I didn't see the point of stuff that just sits on a shelf. Plus, I had to dust it. I also had some of it thrown at me when Mom was angry. I wasn't a fan of the throwing or the items being thrown.

John walked down to the dumpster and rescued what he could. They lived on that living room shelf in their apartment until my mother passed away. Now, I have two of those stoves on a shelf in my sunroom.

My stepdad was a good dad, and he was an amazing grandfather during the short time that he was in my son's life. After my son was born, I went back to school to get my Master's degree. My mom and John babysat my son. They took him everywhere with them: to the mall, to the grocery store, everywhere. My stepdad even let my son "help" him build a trellis. Unfortunately, my son's time with my stepdad was too short. He died when my son was three.

1986 | One of these Afternoons

We were on his bed. The door was closed. The Eagles Greatest Hits CD, our go-to make-out soundtrack, was on the stereo, and RJ's mouth had found that perfect spot on my neck, the triangle of lust. "You have no idea what that does to me!" I said while inhaling the scent of Tide from his shirt.

"Oh, but I do. That's why I'm doing it." He looked up long enough to say that and then went right back to that magic spot.

I had genuine feelings for this boy, as real as they could be when I was 15, but because I was chasing normal, I was dating his best friend, Rickthedick (not his real name). He had a "normal" family, with married parents and everything. RJ, like me, had divorced parents and all the drama that goes with that. So, even though I liked him so much more, I was officially the dick's girlfriend.

RJ and I went to the same school and rode the same bus. That's where we met, the bus stop, on the first day of tenth grade. I was still sad that my summer boyfriend had gone back to his home state. Florida was just a place to vacation for him. Once I got to talking to RJ, though, I wasn't sad anymore.

Now, in RJ's room, I was not thinking of Summer Boy at all. I was just thinking about how badly I wanted to be RJ's girlfriend and do the thing that I had never done before. So, when he looked at me with those deep brown eyes and asked, "You want to?" I answered the only way I knew I had to.

"Do you have a condom?" I was really hoping the answer was yes.

It wasn't. The answer was, "Don't you want to take a chance?"

A chance? My official answer was, "Um, no." What went through my head was the fact that my mom took a chance when she was a teen and ended up with my brother, a kid she no longer had custody of by choice, a shitty, abusive marriage, and me, the baby she became pregnant with while she was on the pill. No. No chances here, sir.

This irritated RJ. I thought it was blue ball frustration. I would learn more later. "Can you at least blow me?"

Again, "Um, no" was my official answer, but my brain went back to that damn recliner at my grandmother's house in Peoria, IL. This was where I had first been forced to perform fellatio on my step-uncle at age two.

This was not the answer RJ wanted. "Come on! I'll do it to you, too!"

Oh god. This was not the consolation prize he thought it was. I instantly thought of how disgusting I felt. I was gross. Dirty. I couldn't let his face near there. Couldn't we just keep going with this neck and Eagles thing? My verbal reply was, "Um, no. I need to shower and stuff."

RJ was very accommodating. "My bathroom is right there! You can use my shower." He jumped up, opened his bedroom door, and pointed towards the bathroom.

Spoiler alert: I didn't have sex, oral or otherwise, with RJ that day or any other day. I was disappointed because I had wanted him to be my "real" boyfriend and be the first.

Shortly after that, someone clued me in on something I did not know about the whole RJ and Rickthedick situation. They had a bet. I'm not sure how much money was at stake, but it didn't matter. Whoever had sex with me first was the "winner." No one won that bet. It was never going to be "real," anyway.

1986 : The Magic of Alcohol

Way before I knew about SSRIs or other anxiety meds, I was introduced to my friend alcohol. Like a lot of teens in the 80s, I had easy access to intoxicating drinks. I tried wine coolers, beer, and sips of my stepdad's liquor, but I never got drunk, for real drunk, until the drama club Sea Escape cruise.

Growing up in South Florida, cruises were pretty common. Sea Escape was a one-day cruise to nowhere, and it was my first cruise. My friends Marilyn, Theresa, and I were taking a drama class as an elective during our freshman year. We were not really into it, but we were into fun. When our teacher said that anyone taking a drama class could go on the Sea Escape with the drama club, we signed up. And, since our parents were all typical 80s parents, they signed the permission slips and handed over the cash.

Marilyn, Theresa, and I set up camp on the deck. We did not splurge for the optional room for the day. We made good use of the free lockers and public showers. So, we spent most of the day in lounge chairs on the deck with SPF hell suntan oil on. When the waiter came around and asked us if we wanted a drink, we ordered piña coladas, thinking they would probably be virgin drinks. Nope. We got the real deal. That's when we learned the beauty of international waters.

I'm not sure how many piña coladas we had or how long we sat in the sun, but I know we had a great day. We were continuously buzzed, and no one puked. It was a win-win.

Alcohol became my go-to social lubricant after the cruise. The first time I had sex, I was drunk. I was 15 and had two wine coolers. They were citrus wine coolers, and they went down easily. I had just met the young man who would deflower me. He was a friend of a friend. We got flirty in the car on the way to South Beach. We were going clubbing on Washington Avenue in Miami. I felt so cool.

When we got to the club, the only one that would let people under 18 in, this guy and I engaged in some dancing that would have gotten us kicked out of the prom. Finally, he suggested we go back to our friend's car, a Buick Regal. He had a condom, and I was tired of not knowing what sex was like. It hurt, and I cried. It was horrible and not John Hughes movie-like at all. Would I have done any of this if wine coolers had not been involved? Probably not. But I still wouldn't say I was forced or anything like that. It was a mistake. Apparently, he agreed.

A few months later, I saw him one time at a mall. I knew it was him. He looked right at me and then looked away. I didn't want to talk to him anyway, but I felt a little hurt by the look on his face. He looked at me like one would look at a spat-out loogie on the sidewalk. Or maybe I'm projecting how I felt about the whole situation. I was with two friends, including RJ, who was still an on-again-off-again boyfriend. I said nothing. I held back my tears and kept talking to my friends about making a record at the booth in the mall. That was a cool thing to do in the 80s; it was kind of like permanent karaoke.

The friend who had introduced me to this guy, also a guy, called me a whore when he found out what happened. That was common in the 80s and beyond. It was always the girl's "fault." Because having sex was "wrong" if you weren't married, but only if you were female. The girl owned the "guilt" of anything sexual. I didn't talk to that friend anymore. I also didn't date for about six months until I met Tom.

1987 | Being Pimped for Weed

"Hey, can I crash at your pad tonight?" Trish asked me as she sat down across from me at Burger King. It was Saturday, and she knew my parents were out of town. I had recently become reacquainted with her after she started going to South Broward in tenth grade. We had first met in third grade, but went our separate ways in seventh grade. Now, here she was, back in my life and giving me free Burger Bundles.

"Sure! My parents don't get home until Monday." I replied while gulping down mini cheeseburgers.

Trish smiled and ran her hands over her bushy blonde hair. "Cool! I'll be there after work. I can bring food. They throw away anything they have cooked when the store closes."

I walked home from Burger King, which was only a couple of blocks from the Atrium Apartments, where we lived. Trish worked at the Burger King where the "getcho ketchup home" incident of 1980 had occurred.

Later that evening, as promised, Trish was knocking at my door with two bags of food and a four-pack of wine coolers. We sat down at my parents' glass dining room table and ate and drank everything. Then, Trish lit up a joint and passed it to me. I wasn't a big pot smoker, but I took one hit and passed it back.

"It's my last one. I gotta save some for the morning," Trish said as she snuffed out the joint on a cheeseburger wrapper. "Oh! I almost forgot! Can I use your phone? There's this guy I want you to meet. He's on the football team at Broward, and he thinks you are cute."

"He knows me?"

"Yes, he's seen you in the halls. He asked me to introduce you guys," Trish said.

My heart fluttered. A boy liked me! I wanted a real boyfriend, not just a crush. I wanted to have an actual relationship. I pictured myself wearing his football jacket and holding hands as we walked down the hall. "Um, ok. It's in the kitchen." I pointed towards our phone, which was on the tiny wooden kitchen table.

I went to the bathroom to brush the cheeseburger residue from my teeth and put on make-up. A BOY was coming over. I needed to look good. I changed into a cute sleeveless denim dress, too. While I was in the bathroom, Trish had discovered the liquor cabinet and had made some sort of sweet, brown drink for each of us. I took a couple of big gulps to calm my nervousness.

And that is when things start to get foggy for me. I remember Assballplayer (not his real name) knocking on the door and Trish letting him in. We sat on the couch with him, and Trish introduced us. I don't remember how we got to my bedroom, though. I mean, I assume we walked there from the living room, but I'm not sure exactly what led up to that.

I remember lying on my twin bed with him and kissing. I was so happy that he liked me. He was cute and a football player. After being a cheerleader, dating a football player was my second-best 1980s high school wish. I never made real cheerleading, but I was a wrestlerette as a freshman. Maybe my dream of dating a football player would come true.

When he unzipped his pants and directed my head toward his pelvis, I figured I should just do this. It would make him like me more. We would be a couple. Plus, I had already done this when Normal made me do it when I was a kid, so I kind of knew what to expect.

After that, I remember a bad taste in my mouth and spitting into a Kleenex. He asked if I was okay as he was zipping his pants and getting up. I felt gross and a little embarrassed. This was not how I expected the evening to go. I did what he wanted, and now he was leaving.

I heard Trish talking to him as I walked across the hall to the bathroom. I rinsed my mouth and brushed my teeth twice. When I came out of the bathroom, he was gone, and Trish was holding a baggy of weed.

"Look what he gave us!" she said with a smile.

"Cool," I said, but I really did not care. I felt really tired and disappointed.

We went to sleep shortly after this. I woke to the smell of Trish smoking a joint. It smelled gross and it was way too early. I sat up in bed and asked her, "What are you doing?"

"Getting ready for work," she replied. She was already in her Burger King uniform, and wet blonde ringlets hung from her head. I went back to sleep after she picked up her backpack and headed out the door.

I didn't think much about that night during the rest of the summer, and I didn't hear from Assballplayer at all. I kind of forgot about the whole incident and figured he would, too.

Nope.

On the first day of my junior year, I was walking to class with my friends, and we walked down the hallway by the cafeteria, where all of the football players and friends sat on a bench before classes started for the day. I locked eyes with him and gave a little wave. He looked at me like someone looks at the bottom of their shoe after stepping in dog crap. I turned away as my cheeks turned red and kept walking.

"SLUT!" One of the guys on the bench yelled, and the other guys laughed.

What? I was really confused. Why was he calling me that? He liked me, right? Apparently not. During my entire junior and senior years, he told anyone who would listen what I had done.

When I started dating Tom later that Fall, he made sure to let him know what a piece of garbage I was. It was fun having THAT talk with Tom.

1988 | **Ease up, Rambo**

I was in the back seat of Dan's car when I met Tom. I was hanging out with Dan, his girlfriend, and a couple of friends. We were driving around the plaza, where everyone hung out back in the day. There was the movie theater with seven screens. There was also a Bennigans, a Burger King, a Baskin Robbins, and, of course, the staple of every Florida plaza, Publix. You name it; this plaza had it.

Dan was parked in the plaza, and this other guy, Tom, walked up to the driver's side window and started talking to Dan. I had never met this person before, but he went to my school. I thought he was cute instantly. He had dark hair (I've never been attracted to blonds, except for Sting) and blue eyes. He looked past Dan and said, "Hi!"

Dan introduced us that night, and within a week, we went on our first date. Our first date involved going to a movie at Ocean Walk on Hollywood Beach. Then, after the movie, we went to the arcade and played a few rounds of video games. We didn't know what to do after that, but we didn't want the night to end, so we went to visit our friend Dale.

I always wonder what happened to Dale. He went to our school for about a year. He lived by himself in a three-bedroom condo on Hallandale Beach. His parents had deposited him there while they stayed mostly in Philadelphia. I never could figure that out. Anyway, Dale's parents had money and gave him a credit card, which he used to buy us alcohol and take us out to dinners we could not otherwise afford. Since I was 16 and broke, and Dale was a super nice guy on top of being rich, I considered him one of my closest friends.

I stayed with Tom for over a year. We were always together. He was my first "real" relationship. We were comfortable together. We slept together, yes, but we also napped together, cooked together (mac and cheese straight from the box), and hung out together every day. Even when we had different classes, Tom seemed to know where to find me. A few times, I would see him looking through the gym door windows and waving at me when I was in dance class. I was flattered that he seemed to like me so much. I wasn't used to this kind of attention.

Then, things got weird when Tom wrecked his car and dropped out of school. Those two things happened right after the other. He was acting like a goofball and racing a friend down a street near our school. This was when they were on their way back from lunch. Anyway, Tom was acting like a teenage boy with a car and trying to show off. He ended up crashing into a pole. He wasn't hurt too bad, but his car was totaled. He had no transportation. Soon after, he dropped out of school.

His employer at the time was like a father figure to him, and this nice man bought him a motorcycle. We continued to date for about a year. Tom got his GED and started taking classes at the community college and working. Tom got clingy with me, and I hate clingy. I'm someone who requires a lot of alone time. He wasn't just clingy; he was possessive. For Christmas, he bought me a large, gold TAKEN charm. He also got defensive when other boys talked to me and immediately claimed me by saying, "She's my girlfriend." I'm no one's possession. I broke up with him.

Tom could not accept that and would follow me places. Once, my friends and I went to a park before a football game to hang out and have a beer or two. In the 80s, teens could purchase alcohol pretty easily. Anyway, Tom showed up. He had followed me and my friend there. He even followed us through a McDonald's drive-through. When we got to the park, he followed me all around, insulting me. Of course, he called me a whore. That was the insult of the day. When he did this, one guy in our group of friends decided to speak up. This person was someone I was never really close to, and he was one of the last people I expected to come to my rescue, but he did. He walked right over to him and said, "Ease up, Rambo!" Everyone laughed because Tom was wearing camo shorts. He finally left.

I didn't see Tom again until we were in our early 20s. We were friends for a bit, and he helped me through a hard time in my life. Tom was a good guy and still is. We were both just too young for that kind of relationship.

1988–1989 | Will and Me

He was walking into the newspaper room, and I was walking out on my way to "sell ads" with my friend. My head turned on its own to look at him as he passed. "Well, hello!" I said before I could catch myself. He turned and smiled. I walked back in.

There was something old-fashioned and a bit dangerous about his vibe. We didn't use the word vibe in the 80s, but that is what it was. He looked like he stepped out of the 40s, with slicked-back hair and a button-down shirt. Not the jeans and t-shirt type boy I was used to seeing.

I found him irresistible.

He went to Mrs. N's desk to have her sign a form allowing him to take newspaper without taking Journalism 101. I had done the same thing the year before. No one wanted to take the yawn-worthy 101 class. We just wanted to write. Some of us also just wanted to have that open pass to leave campus to sell ads. Since the Newspaper class was fourth period, that ad-selling time bled into lunchtime and provided a siesta-worthy lunch break.

After he left, I walked up to Mrs. N's desk and asked, "Who is that? Is he going to be in our class?"

She looked up at me and raised her eyebrows. "You're too old for him, Lisa. Besides, don't you have a boyfriend?" I was and probably still am two years older than Will. I had already started thinking about breaking up with Tom.

I rolled my eyes and said, "Yes, but I'm going to break up with him. He is so clingy and boring. He never lets me have any alone time!" I wasn't lying. Tom had wanted to be with me every second that I wasn't in school or working, and sometimes, he showed up at Publix when I was working.

The following year, Will and I were finally in the same class, and I had finally broken free from Tom. I let Will know in some not-so-subtle ways that I had a crush on him. Will asked me out to lunch. I never enjoyed eating in front of boys, but I wanted to spend time with him, so I went.

At the end of class, we walked across the street to Sizzler. I ordered a salad and water. I didn't want him to think I was a fat-ass. Being overweight was one of the worst things a 1980s teen girl could be. I also didn't want him to go broke feeding me. Back then, if a guy invited you out, he paid.

Will and I sat at a table together for the 20 minutes we had left of our lunch break. We talked a little about the shooting that had occurred in the Sizzler parking lot on the first day of school a couple of months before. That's when I first learned that Will knew a lot about guns.

Our next date was a group event at a local small fair. He met me there with his group of friends, and I was there with my friends. My friends and I were seniors, and they weren't thrilled about hanging out with sophomores, but they knew of my fascination with Will. They rolled their eyes but went along.

We had been flirting for about three weeks by this time. We weren't officially a couple, really, but we liked each other's company, and we were attracted to each other, but he had not tried to kiss me. I was wondering if I was too fat or if he was gay. In my little teen mind, those were the only two reasons for the lack of physical contact. I didn't take into consideration that he was only 15 and I was 17. He would never admit this, but maybe he had never kissed anyone.

Well, we got that out of the way on the Ferris Wheel. I've never liked heights, so I wasn't faking it when I got scared every time the wind shook our little car. He put his arm around me. I turned to look at him, and all the awkwardness suddenly left. Our lips touched, and from that moment on, we could not keep our hands off of each other.

My parents left me home alone while they traveled. This was part of a normal Gen-X upbringing. We lived in an apartment building with many nosy old people, so I never attempted to have a party, but I did sneak Will in after the old people were asleep. By this time, I had been on the pill for a couple of weeks. I had gone to a doctor by myself and gotten them. I really could not have had that kind of conversation with my mom.

We were under my yellow-flowered comforter, kissing and exploring each other's bodies. Things were really heating up, and I reached down and unbuttoned his pants. He asked if I had a condom. I didn't, and I told him I was on the pill. Will was a little worried about us not using a condom. I assured him that the pill would work just fine. I pulled off my panties, tossed them on the floor, and got on top of him. I forced him, sort of. He didn't complain.

We spent most of that school year having sex EVERYWHERE. Most of the time, we were in the back seat of my Chevy Chevette, but sometimes we were on the beach, in a park, or one time, on the steps of city hall. We really could not stay away from each other.

Unless we were "arguing." That is the word he used. By arguing, I mean he was slut-shaming me. After we began having sex, he got angry that he was not my first. Assballplayer had informed him about the summer blowjob seventeen months earlier, and he knew I had been with Tom during our relationship. On the regular, Will would call me a whore and tell me I deserved to be punished. Then, he would sort of get over it for a bit, and we were all over each other again.

One day, he showed me how serious he was about this whole punishment thing. Will held the knife out to me, holding the blade with the handle toward me, almost like he was concerned for my safety. We were standing in front of the bike racks at the library in Hollywood, Florida, a meeting place for us since we both lived within a few blocks of it. I had run over from my apartment across Hollywood Boulevard right after he called me and told me we needed to talk. There I was, staring at the knife and looking at the boy I thought I was in love with.

"Cut yourself," he said, looking into me with those serious brown eyes. I looked up at his combed-back light brown hair and down at his buttoned-up shirt.

I looked away and looked down at my Keds and the dirty sidewalk. I could feel the tears starting already. I ended up crying a lot during my senior year of high school because of this "relationship." I gave him a look of confusion, so he clarified.

"To prove you love me. You lied to me. How do I know you really love me?" I had denied the whole blowjob thing to everyone as soon as the rumor started spreading the year before. I felt guilty and finally admitted the truth to Will recently. He was not very forgiving.

He held the knife closer to me. I was ready to cut myself. I wanted Will to be nice to me and stop getting angry about things that happened before I even met him. I didn't understand his anger and his judgment. I thought maybe cutting myself would make this all stop. I reached for the knife and put the blade to my arm.

Will grabbed the knife back quickly. He didn't allow me to scratch myself, much less cut myself. "I just wanted to see if you would do it." He folded the knife into the handle and put it in the pocket of his khakis. Then he grabbed me and gave me a hug and a kiss. I felt so relieved.

The judgment and name-calling didn't end. There were many more "arguments," as he called them. I wasn't the one starting them, though. I never knew what would set him off. We would be out together, having a great time, and his eyes would go cold, and it would all start again. I was a liar and a whore. I probably would've burned myself at the stake if he told me to.

I didn't see him most of the summer before I left for FSU. His parents made sure of that. To them, I was "that girl." I was the older girl who was going to ruin their precious youngest child. They took him to North Carolina, to their other home. We talked on the phone here and there, but long-distance calls were still expensive, and cell phones and texting did not exist. I did what any sane, normal, love/lust-struck teen girl would have done in 1989. I went to the local Delta ticket office and bought tickets to Charlotte, NC.

Will told me to do this. He told me there was a way I could fly in, and he and an older local friend would pick me up, and then I could stay in a shed and his parents would never find out. IN A SHED. And I was OKAY with this. I was an idiot. It's a good thing I had a best friend who would not let this shit happen.

I paid cash for the tickets. I had to. I didn't have credit cards yet. They were nonrefundable. I made up a story for my parents about how I was going with some girls, including the one who ended up saving me from myself to MGM Studios (now called Disney's Hollywood Studios) in Orlando. I thought I was so smart.

I wasn't. One night, I walked in from working my evening shift at Woolworths in the Hollywood Mall, and my mom was waiting for me in my room. She wasn't as angry as she was the night she had found my birth control pills, but she was definitely not happy with me. Mom told me to sit down, so I did. She explained to me that Theresa had called her while I was working and told her about my whole plan to sneak away to North Carolina. At that moment, I was SO MAD at Theresa and even madder at my mom and Will's parents. Why were they keeping us apart like this? We were in LOVE!

At least, I thought we were. I was very naïve. In addition to regularly slut shaming me, Will liked to tell me huge lies about what he was up to when we weren't together. He had me believing that he worked for a law enforcement agency at the age of 16. He told me he worked for an agency I will not name, in case this was all true, buying guns so they could arrest the people selling the guns to minors. I'm shaking my head at my young self. I mean, how could I have believed this nonsense? A 16-year-old federal agent?

In my defense, Will did act the part. One Saturday, he invited me to a gun show, followed by a trip to a gun range. Will was helping a teacher at our school buy guns for self-defense. I picked Will up that Saturday morning in my Chevy Chevette after calling in sick to work. We went to the teacher's house first so he could show her where to place the guns for easy access in case of a home invasion. Seeing him in this authoritative role made me believe he really was in law enforcement. After our visit to the teacher's home, she went with us to the gun show and to the gun range where she pretended to be our mom. She signed permission slips for us to shoot at the gun range. This is how I learned to fire a gun.

After being away for the whole summer after my senior year, Will's family finally returned to Hollywood a few days before I left for FSU. I'm surprised his parents gave us that long together. I fully expected not to see him before college. We spent those last evenings reminding each other of our fabulous chemistry. It was like he was never away.

I cried all the way to FSU even though Will and I had promised each other to call and write letters. That is all we could do in 1989. We were having a long-distance relationship, and it sucked. This was before Facetime and texting and social media. We had to call each other on prehistoric phones with cords. We had to write letters on paper, with pens, and mail them via the U.S. Dinosaur Service. It was not a good time to be in love from far away, especially as a teen.

Our "love" finally ended because Will forgot my birthday. Yes, because he forgot my birthday, not because he was abusive, but because he couldn't even be bothered to make a phone call or send a card. Being away from Will made me think about why I was putting up with his nonsense. I was already thinking of ending the relationship, but then he forgot my birthday. That made me so mad. I sent him a Dear Will letter.

He called me when he got it, crying and begging me to stay with him. At one point, he told me, "My mom thinks I'm crazy for begging you like this." His mom always hated me. Partly because she was a pruney-faced old bitch, and partly because Will told her EVERYTHING. She knew we had sex, and she knew it wasn't my first time. She should have been nominated for an Emmy for acting like she tolerated me while referring to me as "that girl" when I wasn't around. I don't miss her.

I went home from FSU for Thanksgiving and, like a lot of new high school graduates, I went to visit my old teachers since they were in school while our break had already started. Theresa and I were walking around, stopping by classrooms to say hello, when we ran into him. Somehow, Will was out in the hall while everyone else was in class and ended up walking right toward us. My chest hurt instantly, and I kind of felt like I was going to cry.

"Hi," I said, standing about three feet away from him and looking up at his brooding eyes.

"Hey! I like your hair," he said with a smile, obviously lying. My hair was short and curly. I looked like someone's weird aunt.

"Really? Christine gave me a home perm in our dorm. I didn't think you would like it," I smiled, holding in tears. I had missed him, and it hurt. Why could we not just have a normal relationship?

"Yeah, it looks nice," Then we stared at each other, not knowing what to say. I think it was Theresa who broke the silence.

"Well, I gotta get going. I have to work tonight," Theresa said. I don't think she really had to work, but she was my ride and my ride-or-die, so she knew I needed help getting away.

"Oh. Okay. We gotta go! Bye," I wanted to hug him, but I knew I couldn't. I might not let go.

We turned to walk in separate directions and both turned our heads at the same time and looked at each other one last time. I have not seen or talked to Will since then, but he shows up in my dreams regularly.

1990 | Nice Guy Rebound

I jogged the four aisles from the pet department to the sporting goods section. "Oh my god! Can you help me for a second?" I said to Ed, the sporting goods guy who came in early on Sundays like I did.

Ed was an introverted, sort of gruff, dark-haired young man who worked in the with me at Woolworth. When I say young man, I mean he was four years older than me, 21 to my 17. I liked that about him. Since I was in the pet department, right next to sporting goods, I chatted with Ed frequently.

Ed was in charge of helping people buy the sporting items that were locked away under glass, like rifles and ammo. The sporting goods department was also in charge of making keys. This seemed odd to me because keys didn't seem to relate to any sport, but whatever. I focused on my job in the pet department, or at least I did when there was not a hamster massacre.

Ed followed me over to the glass hamster cage that had sent me running. Inside, there was a dead, eyeless hamster and a very much alive hamster. Ed got a small shovel and a bag and removed the dead guy. I stayed about five feet back and grimaced the whole time. "Why would that happen?" I asked.

"They're mean," Ed said and took the bag away.

Ed and I developed a friendship after that. On Sundays, we would sometimes go on break at the same time and walk around the small Hollywood Mall. Along the way, I stopped to admire a pair of boots in the shoe store window. One Sunday morning, before I left for FSU, I opened the cabinet in the pet department to find those boots gift-wrapped.

But I could not date Ed. I was still fixated on Will at this time, hoping to make him stop mistreating me and love me. I had my head up my ass.

When I went away to college, Ed kept in touch. He called me and gave me his calling card number so I could call him, too. He also sent me a care package every week. It was a Happy Wednesday gift, and it was filled with things to make dorm life less of the living hell it was to an introvert like me. One box contained some good toilet paper and a huge jar of peanut butter. Other times, it was silk pajamas and candy. And this was before I was dating him.

Of course, I started dating him. Right after Will completely forgot my birthday — after I put up with his 1950s patriarchal nonsense. I had found a nice guy.

Ed was one of very few people to meet my brother, Tony. Since Tony and I grew up in separate homes, most of my friends thought I was an only child. Only Theresa, Hillary, and Jon had met my brother before Ed. I filled Ed in on Tony's life, so when we visited my brother at his home, Ed knew what to expect.

When we pulled up, Ed's headlights illuminated a scene straight out of *Joe Dirt*. Two Rottweilers were chained to the porch of my brother's trailer. They started snarling and barking as soon as we walked towards the home. Tony flung open the door to yell at the dogs and let us in. Ed and I rushed up the unfinished wooden steps past the dogs and into my brother's living room/dining room/kitchen.

"Welcome!" my brother said while hugging me. I introduced him to my boyfriend, Ed, and Tony shook his hand. "Have a seat!" Tony gestured to what looked like a typical Rent-A-Center living room. He smiled proudly as though he had just earned his Jerry Springer frequent guest card.

Ed and I sat on a plaid fabric loveseat and leaned forward with our elbows on our knees. "Where's the baby?" I asked. My brother's new wife had just had a son, my brother's first baby, after several pregnancy scares with other women. Tony always referred to condoms as "swimming with a wetsuit."

"Ruth took him to Sawgrass. She wanted to do some shopping." I nodded as if I didn't think that taking a one-week-old baby to the Sawgrass Mills outlet mall was a horrible idea. But I was only 19 and not really into babies, so what did I know? "She should be back soon!"

I handed Tony the present that Ed and I brought for little Jeremy. I was excited to meet my nephew and hoped he would get back soon. Tony took the present and set it on an end table for Ruth to open. I guess opening presents was a mom's task.

Just then, the door swung open, and a large woman with a goofy smile stomped in. The living room floor shook with each step she took toward the bassinet. She dropped Jeremy into it from about a foot up. I cringed. I wasn't a baby expert, but I knew they were fragile.

Ruth put the large purse she was carrying on the floor and grabbed the present from the table. She smiled at me, and my brother said, "This is Lisa, my sister." Ruth hugged me and sat down with the present.

It always felt weird for Tony to refer to me as his sister. We did not grow up together. I always felt more like an only child.

Ruth opened the present, and little Jeremy started fussing in his bassinet. "Do you want to hold your nephew, Lisa?" Ruth asked, holding a light blue bow in her hand.

"Um, sure." I was a little nervous to pick him up. I had no experience with babies, really, and I didn't want to break him.

"Put your hand under his head," my brother instructed me. I slid my left hand under his head and my right under his back and picked up his tiny body. I sat next to Ed and held Jeremy.

Ruth thanked us for the onesie and padded rattle that had been in the box. "He'll love these," she said and sat them back on the table. Ruth winced as she moved in her seat. Looking at Ed, she announced, "They cut me when I had him. It fucking hurts."

I nearly stopped breathing in my attempt not to roll my eyes. Of all the people for my brother's former prostitute wife ("Hey, she supported herself on the streets!" My brother, bragging about Ruth to our mom) to talk about her episiotomy with. I really didn't want it to be the most normal, professional guy I had ever dated. He handled it well, nodding and agreeing that it sounded painful while she used her hand to show him just how they had cut her.

We didn't stay long, telling the new parents that we didn't want to keep them from resting. Really, I think we were done hearing about Ruth's vagina. Tony walked us out to the car, yelling at the dogs as we passed them. "Maybe you could bring Momsie next time." That's what he called her.

"Uh, yeah. I'll ask her," I said, knowing that she "wanted nothing to do with that mangy son and his whore wife." She often said she "wouldn't touch a doorknob Ruth had touched." I knew mom wouldn't come to visit her first grandchild.

Ed and I got in his car and got out of there. "That's my family," I said to him while rolling my eyes. Ed chuckled and continued driving. That was the last time I saw my brother. He died in 2021.

1991 | Group Therapy

I walked the short distance from my room to the front door, staring down at the beige carpet as I walked. My mom and John were sitting on the couch watching *Wheel of Fortune,* and they turned to look at me. "I'll be home in a couple of hours," I told them as I put my hand on the door.

"Where are you going," my mom asked. I didn't really want to tell them, but since I was still living in their apartment at the age of 19, I knew I should.

"Therapy. I found a therapy group for survivors of sexual abuse." With Ed's support, after he witnessed my drinking and put up with emotional abuse from me, I decided to do what my mother should have done for me and for herself a long time ago. I found help. I wanted to stop carrying around this abusive baggage and stop swinging it at Ed.

John looked back at the TV and away from me at the door. He was from the We-Don't-Talk-About-That Generation. My mom's face looked a little red, so I knew she was forced to see the consequences of her parenting once again. "Oh," she said. "Do you think that will help?"

I opened the front door and put my hand on the handle for the screen door. "I don't know, but I have to try." I waved at both of them and stepped onto the welcome mat outside as I pulled the door closed while holding the screen door open.

"I hope you find peace, Lisa," my mom said as I closed the door.

That urked me a bit. She said it like I was troubled. Full stop. Her tone told me that she was once again not taking any responsibility for abusing me herself and not protecting me from the predators in our lives. I let the screen door slam and walked to my car.

I got in my little black Nissan Sentra and turned the air on full blast, waiting for the fog to clear from the windows and my glasses. In Florida, in the summer, the humidity never lets up, not even in the evening. I was a little nervous to be on my way to share my story with a group, but it was my only affordable option. I could not afford one-on-one therapy.

I met a lot of interesting women in this group, and one of them became a good friend. Karen was older than me, but we had a lot in common, and we talked on the phone frequently. Like many of the women in the group, her father was her abuser. All of the women in the group seemed to have some kind of coping mechanism. Mine was humor. I cracked a joke whenever things got too serious. Another woman in the group coped with her abuse by having sex with a lot of different people. She actually had a frequent tester card at the HIV clinic. That is what she told us. Another woman, who was very quiet and didn't share often, confided that she had her first orgasm with her father. She coped by not having sex very often with her husband and avoiding orgasm when she did. Hearing those other stories made me grateful that my father did not do this to me. Even though I was first abused at two, I felt like my abuse by my step-uncle and Rod was not as bad as being abused by a relative.

Karen was in the hospital a few months after I met her. I had talked to her on the phone, and it sounded like she could use some company, so on a Saturday morning, after a night out drinking too much wine with friends, I went to the hospital to visit her. Ed drove me there as we had plans for lunch later. I wasn't prepared for what I saw.

It's not like being in a medical facility was new to me. I had seen my mom in a hospital bed a couple of times with IV tubes in her arms. It didn't bother me. But this woman had a feeding tube in her nose besides the standard IV tubes. This freaked me out. I felt nauseated as soon as I saw it, and then I felt dizzy. I told her, "I'll be back," and I walked out of the room as calmly as I could so I would not upset her.

As I walked back to the waiting room where Ed was waiting for me, I stared down at the hospital floor. I told myself, "It's okay to pass out here. There are doctors and nurses everywhere." Somehow, I did not faint. I made it back to the waiting room and sat down on the floor. I hyperventilated and dry-heaved. Ed sat on the floor next to me and put a trash can in front of me, telling me that I had drunk too much the night before. After a few minutes of this, the cold sweat started, and the nausea went away. I had no idea what had happened, but I was glad it was over. I vowed never to visit anyone in the hospital again.

I stopped going to therapy nine months after I started. Part of the reason I stopped was financial and part of it was that I thought I was fine. Compared to the other women, my abuse was nothing. That is what I told myself. I wasn't fine. I continued to treat Ed poorly, doing things like getting drunk and kissing someone else on New Year's Eve right in front of him, and then I broke up with him for someone else.

1993 | Coulda Shoulda Been Adopted

I was living in Miami with the man I chose over Ed, the man who would become my first husband and the father of my son. I was twenty and feeling independent. I worked full time and went to school full time. On the weekends, usually on a Saturday, I would visit my mom and stepdad in Hollywood.

On one particular Saturday, I met Mom at the Rainbow Café, a cute little restaurant in downtown Hollywood that was used in the movie *Cape Fear*. We sat there in a booth near the salad bar, and looked over the menu while sipping our Diet Cokes. We both decided on the soup and salad bar special. After we got our salads, we sat back down, and my mom began to talk about my father, the biological one, not my stepdad.

I really think that on some very hidden private level, my mom knew that her parenting style was abusive. I understand how she got this way as her own mother did things like make her wear her dead brother's coat rather than buy her a new one. Mom's brother, Johnny, had died in a horrible farm accident when Mom was eight and he was sixteen. His coat wasn't even the right size for her.

I get that Mom didn't have a good role model. I would have been more forgiving if she had ever admitted this or apologized. That wasn't her style. Instead, she liked to make herself look like the better parent by telling me horrible things about my father. From what I had heard from Tony, our father was also abusive, so she wasn't lying. But she wasn't admitting to her own faults.

On this Saturday afternoon, she told me that my dad sent a lawyer to the hospital after she had me to try to get her to sign adoption papers.

They separated when she was eight months pregnant with me. I mostly know her side of the story, though I have heard that she threw a punch bowl at my father's head at some point. Mom admitted to this, stating that he deserved it for abusing her and cheating on her once again. Really, it's a miracle that I am here because they hated each other by this time, and my mom was on the pill. Since my birthday is in September, my only explanation for being here is that the magic of Christmas made them have sex one more time.

I wasn't conceived in a loving marriage. I definitely was not wanted by either of them. If abortion had been legal when my mom had become pregnant with my older brother and forced to marry my father, you would not be reading this. Neither of my parents was great with kids. My father tried to say I wasn't his. When I was born, he saw me and said I looked "oriental." I guess that is why he wanted to give me up for adoption. Also, I bet he didn't want to pay child support.

My mother put her salad fork down and took a drink from her Diet Coke. She looked at me as if to say, "Can you believe this shit?" She spoke proudly about how she said no to my father and the lawyer and kept me. I bit my lips together so that I wouldn't say what I really thought about all this. I had learned to stifle my feelings long ago as my mom was an I'll-give-you-something-to-cry-about parent.

I flashed back to all the beatings and the times my mother raged about something stupid and broke any glass object in sight. I thought about being sexually abused throughout my life. I thought about being afraid to take the SAT for Duke. I thought about how I focused on boys to get love instead of focusing on school. All of this was going through my head, and I wanted to say, "WHY DIDN'T YOU?? Why didn't you give me up for adoption? Do you know what kind of people adopt babies?? People who want them. People with enough money to care for them!"

Instead, I said, "Thank you for keeping me," and poked my fork into a cherry tomato.

1993 : Young Love

I'm not sure how he got to me so quickly, seeing as how he was in the passenger seat. He must have flown over the top of the car because before the door even fully closed, his hands were around my neck and shaking me while yelling, "DON'T FUCKING SLAM MY DOOR!"

The door in question was attached to my boyfriend Richard's new (to him) BMW. It had stalled for the third time, and I was pissed, mostly at myself for not knowing how to drive a stick. We were in the parking lot of our apartment building and I demanded he teach me to drive his car after we got back from Denny's at 9:00 am. He was working the third shift at the time, and he had not been to bed yet. He was a wee bit short on patience.

When the car stalled for the third time after I had barely gotten out of the parking space, I flung open the car door, got out, and SLAMMED the door with all of my might. That is what prompted the parking lot choking.

You would think I would have been terrified, but I wasn't. I was mad. I swung my purse around and hit Richard as hard as I could: "GET YOUR HANDS OFF OF ME!"

He actually did. He took a couple of steps back and told me to "GET OUT!"

I shook my head. "What?" Get out of what? We were outside in a parking lot surrounded by half-dead hedges.

"Get your stuff and get out of the apartment! I can't be with you." He turned to check the driver's side door for damage, rubbed his finger on a scratch that had already been there, and then walked towards the apartment building we had lived in for six months in North Miami.

My heart dropped. In seconds, I went from super angry to sad. I followed him into the lobby.

"Oh, come on! It was just a fight. You need sleep. I'll leave you alone. I'm sorry!" I was fighting tears as I tried to reason with him.

He turned towards me, leaning in, "NO! GET OUT!"

I could not understand how he could end our relationship so suddenly over something minor like a slammed door. By this point, we had been a couple for two years. I first met him in biology class in college. I felt close to him quickly. He even witnessed one of my panic attacks early on.

It seemed like all of the students were excited about this lab except for me. The professor sat us in alphabetical order and Richard was two rows in front of me. Everyone in the class had a microscope on the table in front of them, and a lancet, alcohol swab, and Band-Aid next to the microscope. We were going to find out our blood types. What could go wrong?

I hadn't even pricked my finger yet when it started. First, the nausea came, and then the heart palpitations. I looked around the room, and some goober in my class was showing everyone his bloody finger. Then, I noticed everyone had blood on their fingers. My first thought was, "Can I catch AIDS if I get someone's blood on me?" I started hyperventilating, and so I dropped my lancet on the table and walked quickly to the bathroom down the hall. Once I was out of everyone's sight, especially Richard's as he had followed me out of class, I dry heaved and splashed cold water on my face. Once I was better, I walked out and almost walked into Richard, who was waiting outside of the bathroom.

"What's wrong? Are you sick?" he asked while putting his hand on my shoulder. I just nodded, sparing him the details. This was when I started to feel like we were really a couple. I felt like he was looking out for me.

He definitely wasn't looking out for me after I slammed his car door. I took the elevator with him in silence, trying to process what had happened. Yesterday was a normal day. I had gone to the Aventura Mall to buy Christmas presents. It was December 15, and I was done shopping but still had to wrap the Elizabeth Taylor perfume I had gotten for my mother. It was a normal, Florida Christmas experience. Today, though, was not normal.

I walked into our bedroom and pulled my floral Jordache duffle bag and suitcase from the closet. I began packing through tears, stopping to wipe them with my hands. I'm not sure where he went while I was packing. He wasn't there. I felt like I was going to vomit my waffles. I stopped to call the only person who always brought comfort to my life—Fran.

She answered, sounding annoyed by the phone. This was before caller ID, so you never knew who was calling. "He's kicking me out! He tried to choke me!" I sobbed and coughed into the cordless phone while I took clothes off of hangers and shoved them into my bags.

Fran told me it was good I was leaving, then. These situations, meaning domestic violence, never got better. She told me to repeat to myself, "I'm a good person, and I deserve better."

I kept repeating that in my head as I grabbed my toiletries and as many shoes as would fit in my suitcase. I'd have to come back to get the rest. I hoped by then Richard would have gotten some sleep and realized he'd made a mistake.

I moved back into my parents' two-bedroom, two-bathroom apartment in Hollywood. They were thrilled, of course, especially my 68-year-old stepdad. I had been out from under their roof for two years, working full time and paying my own bills, and now I was back, and I was a sobbing mess.

"Whadya cryin' over that asshole for?" My stepdad asked me when I showed up in tears with my luggage. "He did ya a favor!"

I nodded and looked down at the carpet as I carried my bags to my room. I didn't have the energy to argue. At that moment, I was too sad to have energy for anything. I had lost my boyfriend and my home ten days before Christmas.

I didn't eat that day or the next morning. I forced myself to drink some water before calling my therapist's office. I hadn't seen her in a couple of years but I really felt like I needed to talk to someone. Luckily, she had a cancelation and an opening that morning. I brushed my hair, threw some water on my face, and put on shorts and a T-shirt.

I went out to my car to drive to the therapist's office. Or at least that is what I thought I was going to do. When I turned the key in the ignition the car would not start. I heard a clicking noise whenever I turned the key. I knew what that meant. I wasn't going anywhere with a dead battery.

I went in and told my stepdad, John, about the battery. He had just gotten back from riding his bike to the beach and back.

John walked out to the parking lot with me, carrying a handkerchief and wiping sweat from his bald head and forehead. He pulled his huge, green 1978 Lincoln Town Car up to my car and pulled out the jumper cables to start it.

"You need a new battery. Take it up to Sear's," he told me. There I was, driving to the mall in a zombie-like depression to get a new battery for the car. I didn't get a chance to call the therapist's office.

Of course, the battery was going to take a couple of hours to install. There were other people in line in front of me. I had some time to kill, and there was only one thing to do — walk around the mall. It was morning, so the mall was pretty dead. I was glad because I didn't think I could have handled seeing happy couples everywhere. I was already tolerating Christmas decorations and music. I sat on a bench in the mall, put my head in my hands, and took a few breaths.

That's when I smelled the hot pretzels. Suddenly, my stomach kicked my brain and said, "FEED ME!" I walked over to Auntie Ann's and got a huge, salty, hot pretzel, and a Diet Coke. I didn't think I was hungry, but it had been 24 hours since my last meal. I inhaled the pretzel and then walked around the mall some more, checking my watch every five minutes. It was 1993; there were no cell phones, at least not for regular young people.

A couple of days later, John went with me to the old apartment to get the rest of my stuff. He made sure that Richard wouldn't be there because he wanted to hurt him. After I gathered the rest of my clothes, shoes, and books, we went back to Mom and John's apartment. My parents let me live with them through the holidays. Then, John found me an apartment in the complex. It was a one-bedroom, one-bathroom, all to myself. It was the first time and the last time I ever lived alone.

Once I got over the initial sadness from the breakup, I started to feel normal again. Well, as normal as someone like me can feel. I went to work at a call center and interrupted people's dinners to persuade them to activate that Mastercard they got in the mail. Then, when I got home, I read novels and typed papers on my old-school word processor. I was in my last semester of college, working on a BA in English.

I guess you could say I kept busy, partially because I HAD to and partially because I didn't want to think about the failed relationship. I had thought I was going to marry Richard. Since we hadn't spoken since the parking lot choking incident, and since he had not even apologized, I tried to put him out of my head.

I had friends from work to hang out with. My work bestie, Luz, made sure I was out and about. We went out as a group after work and did karaoke and other alcohol-related activities. Of course, there was a cute guy in the mix.

Mike was taking a semester off from college due to a bad case of mono he had suffered at school. He had not been able to play basketball, which messed up his scholarship. Or at least that is what he said. I didn't care. He was tall, with dark hair, and TOO YOUNG. He was only 19 and lived with his parents. I did what any responsible 22-year-old woman with a crush would do; I slipped him shots under the table when we were out with the group. Mike sent me roses on Valentine's Day with a sweet card. Other than one make-out session in a part of our work building that was being remodeled, we never had a chance to date. That's okay because I ran into Richard.

I really wasn't planning on ever talking to Richard again. I started to like having my own place and my freedom. I liked hanging with friends and cute guys. I was doing good. When I put on my graduation outfit, grabbed my cap and gown, and got in the car with my mom, Fran, and Nicole to go graduate from FIU, I wasn't even thinking about Richard.

Of course, I ran right into him after graduation. I was exiting the auditorium at the same time he was. I tried to pretend I didn't see him, but he saw me. He pulled me aside and looked at me with those bright blue eyes, and pulled me in for a big hug. He told me he missed me. I got tears in my eyes.

So, when he asked me to marry him a couple of weeks later, I did what any sane, introverted girl who was sick of meeting new guys would do. I said, "Yes." My parents thought this was nuts, but they did really love the grandson who arrived two years later.

1997 | Before the Ides of March

When I was first pregnant, they got my due date wrong. This is because the nurse assumed that I did not really know exactly when I conceived my son. I did. She was looking at my menstrual cycle and trying to calculate when I ovulated. She assumed I was "normal." Nothing about me is normal, not even my menstrual cycle.

I knew when my son was conceived because a wedding had been involved, not mine. My now ex-husband's co-worker had gotten married a few weeks earlier. Canadians know how to throw a party, and this was a Canadian wedding. The booze was flowing. At the wedding, I had four vodka tonics, a glass of wine, and a glass of champagne. I was drunk. My husband had a few drinks, too. Our judgment skills were a little off. Long story short, we decided it was a "safe" night. We had been married a couple of years; we were not trying for a baby, but not actively not trying either. While our son was a bit of a surprise, he was not an accident.

I knew damn well when my son was conceived. Finally, after much argument and a scary ultrasound where the doctor told me I was going to miscarry because the "sac was too large for the embryo" or something, they finally agreed with me on when the baby was conceived. A due date of March 15 was given. Being an English major, I could not get "Beware the Ides of March" out of my head. That is from Shakespeare's Macbeth. Unlike most English majors, I hate Shakespeare, but I still had to read it, so I still remembered that line. That all went out the window at 7:00 am on March 10.

I was dreaming about having menstrual cramps. In my dream, I had my period, and I was looking all over for a maxi pad. I've never really been a tampon girl. So, since I was wearing moist, uncomfortable underwear in my sleep, I didn't wake up right away when my water broke. It was all just part of the dream.

Until it wasn't. Suddenly, the cramping got a bit too intense, and I realized I was lying in some sort of puddle. I hit my then-husband.

"It's time!" I yelled at him.

"What?" he replied, stretching and yawning.

"My water broke."

That was all I needed to say. I swear he literally jumped out of bed. I waddled to the bathroom, leaking amniotic fluid the whole way. Once I felt like the leak was under control, I grabbed some panties and a maxi pad and continued getting dressed. As if a maxi pad could contain that. HA! I walked over to my closet and grabbed a long, ugly brown dress. I put it on quickly, feeling like I was peeing into the maxi pad the whole time. Then, I went back to the bathroom to change maxi pads. This was insane. I needed a diaper. Finally, my husband persuaded me to just get in the car and stop worrying about my water leaking. So, we did. By the time we got to the hospital, my dress had a huge wet spot on it.

Once we walked into the hospital and explained that I was in labor, things started moving quickly. I was taken to the maternity ward in a wheelchair and brought into a room. I changed into a gown and climbed into bed. That's when that poor student nurse had to deal with me.

I'm all about supporting education. So, when the primary nurse asked me if I would be okay with this student nurse putting in my IV, I said sure. Mistake. I don't have the easiest veins in the world, PLUS I was in pain. This was a horrible combination. The student nurse stuck me three times without finding a vein. Naturally, I yelled, "Can I please have someone who knows what the FUCK they are doing?!" I'm sure that poor student nurse is a wonderful nurse now, and she probably tells this story every Thanksgiving while eating pumpkin pie with her adoring family.

The nurse was not the worst part of my labor experience. It was the asshole doctor on duty. He wasn't my regular doctor. I had a warm, wonderful OB/GYN throughout my pregnancy. I won't use his name, but his nephew was on the show *Full House*, and he was also Aladdin. He told me all of this during exams. I found that to be really neat, the fact that his nephew was mildly famous and that he actually talked to me about such things during exams. That doctor was so awesome. He told me I was glowing and looked beautiful at every appointment. And then I had to see his partner.

At this OB/GYN practice, they made you see other doctors towards the end of your pregnancy because your own doctor might not be on call when you went into labor because no one ever goes into labor during normal business hours. I waddled into the office at about eight months to see Dr. Z. I could tell that Dr. Z was an @$$%&*^; I mean jerk, the minute he walked in because he did not make eye contact with me. He just told me to assume the position. I asked if he could look at a rash I had developed on my bikini line. I thought it was a heat rash since I lived in South Florida, and I had a heck of a gut with this pregnancy. The doctor stood a couple of feet away from me and said, "It's a fungus!"

I was horrified. His alarmed tone made it sound like black mold was going to eat me alive. "How did I get a fungus?" I genuinely thought I had some South American rainforest-level stuff happening.

He stepped back about three feet and said, "I don't know. Get some anti-fungal cream at the drugstore. Also, you might want to start watching your weight. You've gained too much." With that, he walked out of the room. I pulled my paper blanket around me and slid off the table to get dressed.

I had to hold back the tears. I was fat, AND I had a fungus. This was not good. I did what people usually do when they are insulted like this. I went home and ate macaroni and cheese. Lots of it. I shoveled it in my mouth while muttering, "I'm fat, and I have a fungus. JERK."

Guess who was on call when my water broke? Yep. Dr. Z examined me and told me, "Your water didn't really break." I swear he rolled his eyes when he said it.

I rolled them right back. A person CAN TELL when her water breaks. I told him, "Well, then I must have lost control of my bladder in bed, all the way to the bathroom, through two maxi pads, and in the car on the way over here." I wanted to throw my wet, brown dress at him. Jerk.

I labored for 17 hours, and my epidural quit working and needed to be inserted again. Good times. I ended up needing an emergency C-section. Lucky for me, his surgical skills were way better than his bedside manner. I never saw him again, and I don't miss him.

Though the labor and delivery were absolute hell, I am so glad to have my son. He is my soul mate and the only one I can share really dark humor with. I will be writing another memoir about him and my parenting style. Stay tuned.

1996 | Comedy Clusterfuck

My heart was pounding, and I wasn't sure if I was going to faint, vomit, or both as I walked to the stage. It was the Spring of 1996, and I was about to make my dreams come true at Uncle Funny's open mic night in Davie, Florida. I had written some jokes. I suspected they were funny, but I had no idea what to say when I first got to the mic.

"Hello." That was my big opening line. There was absolute silence. I got more nervous, as if that were possible, and squinted at the spotlight. I knew I had to find a way to show them I was funny. I just started my act.

"They say the meek shall inherit the earth, but I think it will be the stupid." Laughter! Oh my god! There was laughter — an enormous sigh of relief. I dared to look towards my first husband, who was recording this magic moment on a tape recorder. We didn't have smartphones yet.

"Everything is geared towards stupid people, right? For example, warning labels." And that was it. I went into my warning label material, and there was a lot of laughter. I had to pause and wait for them to stop laughing. I felt so good after my set. I had stars in my eyes. I just KNEW that I would be on Saturday Night Live someday and maybe have my talk show. It was all going to come together. I just knew it.

It didn't.

About three months after I started doing open mic nights, I got pregnant. I could have still continued to perform while pregnant.

Hell, the baby bump would have probably made me funnier. But I didn't. I got it into my head that moms shouldn't be comedians. Plus, comedy clubs were still smoky back then, and I wanted to avoid breathing that in. So, I took a break. A two-year break. I didn't do another open mic night until my son was over a year old.

I sat at my desk in the shared FAU English Department adjunct office and drank bad cafeteria coffee while grading freshman composition essays. My son was born in March 1997, so I figured starting grad school and teaching two comp courses in the fall of 1997 would be a great idea.

I hadn't planned on doing comedy ever again, and I wouldn't have if it weren't for the nice young gentleman who sat across the office from me. We were chatting away one day, and I told him I did a couple of open mic nights, but now that I was a mom, I wasn't planning on pursuing it.

"Why not?" he asked. "Moms can do comedy." He spoke with a smile and then turned around and kept lesson planning like he didn't just completely drop a bomb in my little life.

I started thinking. The young fella was right. I can do whatever I want. I could do comedy. I can still be famous. I can do this. YES! I went back to the open mic circuit.

I actually got some paying gigs. By paying, I mean I got like $20 a show. I wasn't raking in the dough, but it felt good to be paid. I even scored a local commercial. I thought I was going to be famous.

Then, I had an affair and blew up my own little life.

Brad was a fellow comedian who always seemed to be at the same open mics. I wasn't physically attracted to him at all. But he had a great smile and seemed smart, like book smart. I could have genuine conversations with him, unlike what I was experiencing at home with Richard. Most conversations with my husband ended in, "Pass me the remote." We were not a cerebral match.

But Brad was different in many ways. He was nine years older than me, originally from New England, and had lived in a few different states. He drove a Jeep without a hard top, and he read the newspaper daily. I can't say I was in love with him, but I think I was looking for an escape from my marriage, and he was it.

For about six months.

I told Richard about him immediately, and after a tear-filled argument, I moved out. Brad and I moved in together out of economic necessity. Neither one of us made much money. My son went back and forth from my new home to his father's home. I felt guilty, and I hated the situation, but I also enjoyed being with someone who supported my comedy "career" mostly because he was chasing a comedy career of his own.

He was also chasing a sugar mama. And that was not me. I could barely pay my half of the bills on my teaching assistant salary, let alone his. When he got fired from his day job and ran up a bunch of 976 sex calls on the phone in my name, I kicked him out.

My husband and I separated, and he was really fighting me for custody of our son. There was no way in the world that I wanted to lose my son, so I cut down on comedy. I turned down shows that would take too much time away from my son. I kept doing comedy for years, though, just locally. No one makes it to Saturday Night Live only doing local clubs.

I started falling out of love with my drug of choice, making a crowd of drunk strangers laugh. It became exhausting. I used to hide in the comedy club kitchen after shows because I could not stand all the drunk people trying to shake my hand. One super special man even licked my face after a show. GROSS! I decided I was done with entertaining drunks. I did my last show in 2006. It's the only show I have on video. Well, the camera guy screwed up, so only the last few minutes are on video.

I haven't done stand-up comedy in 18 years, and I'm okay with that. I'm in my pajamas by 8:00 pm instead of pacing backstage and rehearsing my opening line. Now, I prefer to put my jokes in writing. I figure I'm still making people laugh, even though I can't hear them, and I don't have to put up with beer spit on my face.

2000 | My First Imaginary Mayberry

I was sitting in my little black Nissan Sentra with my arm resting out the open window, waiting for the teller to send me the cash I had requested from depositing my paycheck from the Festival Flea Market Mall commercial. I was tired and staring at the tennis court across the street, forgetting that Ned was sitting in the passenger seat. When the machine came to life and spat out the tube with my cash, I waved my hand lazily and said, "Thank you" to the teller.

Ned's laughter brought me back to earth. I looked at him with furrowed eyebrows, not knowing why he was laughing. Then, I pulled out of the bank and took a right to go through the alley that separated the bank from the tennis courts in this part of Hollywood.

"You sounded like a special person." Ned rolled down his window, stuck his hand out, and said, "Thank you" with a slurry voice. I couldn't help but laugh even though I didn't want to. I have always found it highly amusing when people mimic me.

Ned kept going with his scenario. "The tellers are probably back there saying, 'Good for her! She can drive! She has her own bank account!'" Luckily, we were at a red light because that made me laugh until tears filled my eyes. Looking back, it's not funny at all, but at the time, Ned was new in my life, and after knowing him for three months, I was about to move in with him in Fort Myers, Florida.

I met Ned when I hosted a comedy show in Fort Myers a few months before. My friend and fellow comedian, Valerie, had been asked to host but she was traveling as a headliner already, so she called me to ask if she could give my number to the club owner. I was thrilled. I was just starting to get paid for doing comedy and I really hoped to make it a career.

Ned introduced himself to me shortly before the first show. When I first looked into his blank brown eyes, the word "sick" entered my brain. It would take a few months before I learned why that happened. At that point, when I first met him, I ignored my instinct and talked myself into a friendship with him since we seemed to have so much in common.

He was a comedian, too, and he was recently divorced, or so he said. He wasn't performing when I was there, as the shows were being advertised as female comedians only. Women being funny was still a novelty back then. After the show, Ned took me and the headliner out to dinner. Well, he drove us out to dinner. She actually paid.

As we drove from the club to the outdoor mall where we would eat, I looked out the back seat window at the cute houses and clean sidewalks. It was so different from the east coast of Florida. I thought of what it would be like to move there. I hated that I had to get back to the crowded and dirty southeast coast of Florida.

The next morning, when I was driving east on I-75, heading home from that first Fort Myers weekend, my cell phone rang. It was Ned. He kept me on the phone and entertained for the entire two-hour drive home. The only issue with that was the bill that came a month later. This was before unlimited plans and free long-distance.

After that first weekend, we would visit each other on the weekends that Richard had our son. During one of those visits, he sat on the cheap fabric couch in my living room and told me all the ways he could help with my comedy career. When I showed him a ten-minute tape of one of my recent hosting gigs, he told me that he knew the booking agent for the Tonight Show and that he had been on the show a couple of times. I believed him and asked him for the contact information so I could send my tape.

Every time I asked him for the phone number, he had an excuse for why he didn't have it with him. Finally, after I got impatient, I searched online and found the contact information for the person in charge of booking comedians on the Tonight Show.

After taking some deep breaths, I dialed the number. The man who answered was the booking agent himself. I stammered out that I was a friend of Ned's, and he told me to call and see if I could send my demo tape in.

"Who?" he answered after I was done stammering.

Again, I told him Ned's full name and the "fact" that he had been on the show and thought I should send in a tape. His answer shocked me.

"I've never heard of that person in my life."

"Are you sure?" I asked, repeating Ned's name and where he was from.

"Nope, never worked with him. Listen, you seem like a nice person. It sounds like he is lying to you. Be careful. Crazy usually doesn't get better." With that, he gave me his address and told me to send my tape. He did warn me about "being seen before I was ready." I thought I was ready.

I wasn't. I never appeared on the Tonight Show. Even after knowing that he lied, I still ended up moving across the state to live with Ned. The lies didn't stop. He told me stories of going on the road with musicians to open for them. Ned told other people at the comedy club that he and I had bought a house in an exclusive neighborhood. The way he lied made me angry and nervous, but I ended up living with him for four years. I was a broke single mom, and I needed a roommate. We hardly saw each other as he worked nights and I worked during the days. I wouldn't say we had a real romantic relationship or a relationship at all. We tolerated each other until he found someone else.

2000 | UNCLE Bobby

My heart fluttered when he wasn't in his room. I thought maybe I was too late. I finally found him outside, in front of the hospital, sitting on the cement, edging around the bushes, holding his IV pole and smoking a cigarette. Bobby had quit drugs and booze years ago, but smoking was tough to stop, even though it made his breathing more difficult. He was always a thin person, but now he was skinny and pale. His eyes had lost their sparkle. Bobby looked like he was dying. That is what HIV did to a person after nine years in the early 2000s.

Bobby was really surprised to see me; he didn't think I would visit him. I guess he didn't know how important he was to me. I never really told him because that is how I roll. I don't talk about feelings much. Bobby was Fran's brother and Nicole's uncle. Fran took care of me when my mom worked, and I had always considered Bobby an uncle. He was nice and funny, and he did hair.

Bobby gave me a haircut for the first time when I was four. It was the very popular Dorothy Hamill cut. I loved it. And I loved him. I met him after I had already been sexually abused at three. At this time in my life, I was afraid of most men, but not Bobby. He was the first gay man I had met, and he helped me to feel relaxed around most of the gay men I would meet in my life. I told myself that they like men, not girls. So, they won't do those things to me.

I followed him to the elevator and back up to his room. I waited for him to get comfortable and covered in bed before I sat next to him. I knew this was probably my last time seeing him. I told him he was a person who brought peace to my chaotic childhood. Bobby acknowledged that my mom was "always tough" on me. He was one of very few adults in my life to be that honest. I told Bobby that I was separated from my husband and seeing a comedian who lived on the west coast of Florida, which was two hours away. He told me not to move to Ft Myers. Bobby said the distance was good. I should have listened. I ended up spending four years with a compulsive liar who was into weird porn.

I didn't make it to his memorial service about a couple of months later, partly because I am not a funeral person and partly because I was off being an asshole in Fort Myers, where he told me not to move.

Years later, I was talking to Fran on the phone, and she told me that Bobby had told her about my visit to his hospital room. She told me he said, "Lisa is the real deal." And that is all I've ever really wanted to be.

2004 | **A Maltese and Herpes**

Those were the gifts that The Toad (not his real name), a guy I was dating, gave me. He bred his own dogs and was trying to sell the puppies on whatever Craig's List was called in 2004. I think it was Craig's List. My son, who was seven, fell in love with one of the puppies. The Toad let him have one. So, Lola became a member of our family. The Toad then gave me another forever gift — herpes. Well, I guess the disease was the only never-ending gift. Lola died after 15 years. The disease he gave me never will.

It was like a fairy tale gone wrong. I kissed a frog, and he turned into a TOAD, a big warty toad that gave me a painful and embarrassing disease instead of a prince. At first, The Toad was funny, charming, and cuddly. He had been fond of me for years. He told me we had first met at a comedy club where I was performing, but I was living with Ned, and he was in a relationship. The Toad must have been scoping out the next victim because he kept me in mind.

Now, let's fast forward three years or so. I was teaching at a small private school my son was attending, and The Toad's daughter was in my class. Yes, I taught, performed stand-up comedy, wrote, and still managed to be a mom. One word: vitamins. Anyway, back to my unfortunate meeting with The Toad. Whenever he had to come into the classroom for any reason, he was funny and friendly, oh yeah, and trying to sell me a house. As an unsuccessful real estate agent, he was always trying to make a sale. As a teacher living on $25,000 a year, I wasn't buying.

In the summer of 2004, I got lonely. I had recently ended a four-year relationship with Ned, and he had helped me move to a new home. I was living alone for the first time in 12 years and my son was visiting his father for the summer. I got lonely and STUPID. I put my profile on a popular online dating website. I'll find someone to hang out with, I thought, someone to go out to dinner with. Enter The Toad.

His email stood out from the others immediately. The subject line read, "Hot for B's teacher." I knew who it was immediately, and I cringed a bit. My first instinct was to delete the email without reading it. I had heard his daughter talk about his drinking. Out of sheer stupidity, I opened the email. It was, of course, funny and charming. Then, I did something even more ignorant. I asked people for advice. I have learned to go with my gut instinct now. My best friend told me, "Oh, his profile sounds interesting. Give him a chance." When I read it to my mom, she encouraged me to go out with him. "Have a free dinner," she said. Yeah, why not, I thought.

And what a lovely dinner it was. The Toad took me to my favorite Italian restaurant. We had drinks, and drinks, and drinks. Did I mention this guy was a drinker? Oh yeah, and we had some food, too. Anyway, seeing as how I am the only "light-weight" Irish girl ever, I got ridiculously drunk. My judgment skills went right out the window. I signed up for a second date, even though I noticed a half-full bottle of rum in his back seat.

In total, I stayed with him for three months, and that was only because it was a horrific hurricane season, and I was too short and weak to put shutters on the house I was renting by myself. He did this for me. I guess I used him for free dinner AND handyman services. It's okay. Karma bit me good.

Besides being a bad real estate agent who did not sell anything the entire three months I was with him, The Toad also bred his pet Maltese dogs and sold the puppies. I believe this might be called a small-time puppy mill. When we were dating, he had two adult dogs and three cute, fluffy white puppies.

I was a cat person. I had never owned a dog in my life. So, I just sort of tolerated his puppy mill shenanigans and did not ask for a puppy, mostly because I did not want one. My seven-year-old son did, though. He asked for a puppy and The Toad said, "Yes." WITHOUT EVEN ASKING ME. A Maltese puppy who requires regular grooming is not exactly what a single mom living on a teacher's salary needs. I kept her because I figured she was better off with me than being forced to mate with her father. That is what he wanted to do! Mate the girl puppies with their father.

Three months into our "relationship," The Toad took his daughter on a wild, drunken ride, and that was the last straw for me. I had gotten tired of his constant drinking and the way he always wanted to stay over. I had no space. I had no idea about the herpes yet. That knowledge would come with my first outbreak about a few days after I broke things off.

I went to the doctor on Election Day 2004, thinking I had some sort of wicked yeast infection or perhaps a brown recluse bite in just the wrong spot.

Nope. Nothing that easy.

When I first got into my gynecologist's exam room, I explained my spider bite theory to the nurse. I figured a brown recluse must have bitten me in my girly bits to cause this kind of pain. She stifled a laugh and asked me if I had used any new detergents lately. I didn't think that I had, but I usually bought whatever Publix had on sale. The nurse handed me a paper gown and blanket and told me to undress for the doctor.

Dr. S came in and talked to me for a few minutes before telling me to lie back and put my legs in the stirrups. I gritted my teeth and slid my bottom all the way to the end of the table, as the doctor instructed me to, putting my feet in the stirrups. I always feel like I'm either going to fall off of the table or let out the loudest fart ever when I am in this position. Luckily, neither of those things happened.

Dr. S inserted the speculum, telling me, "I'm sorry, Lisa. This might hurt, but I have to see inside."

She was right. "FUCK!" I said.

Dr. S patted my knee and said, "I bet!" Then she asked while shaking her head and sighing, "You have a new partner, don't you? Have you been using condoms?"

I gulped before answering, "No."

"Lisa! What do I have to do!!!" My doctor had told me several times before to use condoms. I had used them as birth control during my nearly sexless four-year relationship with Ned. But once I started taking the pill again, I was totally and completely stupid. I didn't think that anything like herpes would ever happen to me. I thought of the new guy I was dating, The Toad, as a normal divorced man seeking love. I never thought he would give me a disease.

Then my doctor asked me when the last time I had "intercourse" was. I told her Wednesday night (six days earlier) that I had broken up with him over the weekend because he drove his daughter somewhere while drunk. She said that the timing was about right, and it "looks like herpes."

Herpes!! That doesn't go away! SHIT!!!

My doctor was asking her nurse for different instruments and tests. I lay there thinking about The Toad and how I wished I had never met him. Now, I had a disease that would last my whole life. I was staring at the ceiling, regretting the last three months of my life, when I was brought back to reality by Dr. S's voice, "You're not going to like me." And boy, was she right. She jabbed a cotton swab into a very sensitive spot, and I nearly went through the ceiling. I put my hand over my eyes and thought of saying, "There's no place like home," and clicking my heels. Anything to get me out of here. I wished that this was a nightmare.

After that, I was permitted to sit up. My doctor told me she had taken a couple of cultures and that they would call me with the results. However, it looked like herpes. Dr. S gave me some samples of Valtrex and instructions on how to take them. She also gave me a prescription for a year's supply. She told me they cost about $100 per month. There was no generic at that time. I was a single mom who worked as a teacher. There was no way that I could afford my prescription. I wanted to shoot The Toad. No, shooting would be too kind.

After Dr. S dropped the first bombshell on me, that I had herpes, she dropped a bigger bomb. She told me I should get tested for HIV as soon as possible because people who have one STI have a higher chance of having HIV. My heart dropped, and my eyes threatened to tear. I held it in as best as I could. How did I get myself into this situation? I was stupid. I believed I was somehow immune to STIs. I was now being awakened by the spiritual world. It was smacking me across the face and shouting, "Use condoms, you moron!"

As soon as Dr. S left the room, I jumped down from the examining table, put my paper gown and paper blanket in the garbage, and thought about how they were both probably biohazards because I had touched them. I walked over to the chair where my clothes were and picked up my panties. Now, they looked like something that should be in a biohazard container, too. They were no longer my comfy purple undies; they were a weapon. They held a virus that could cause someone else as much pain as I was in.

After I finished getting dressed, I walked to the checkout counter with my bag of Valtrex in one hand and my purse in the other. It was time to pay for the torture. I had insurance, but it was an HMO, Hand Money Over. I had tears in my eyes as I was writing the check. Not only did I just find out The Toad had given me herpes, but there was a chance that I had HIV. Right then, for all I knew, the virus could have been growing inside of me.

I cried as I drove home. I hated The Toad and hated myself for being so naïve. I wished for a Delorean and a mad white-haired scientist to save me. If only I could go back in time and say no to

The Toad. It would be better to be lonely and bored than to have herpes. I really hated that man.

Believe it or not, I actually had an appetite when I got home. I made myself a little sandwich and took my first Valtrex. I gulped it down quickly, hoping that the blue caplet would bring relief. I was too sore to sit normally. I sat at my dining room table, leaning slightly to the right, and ate my sandwich quickly.

When I was done eating, I looked at all of the paperwork that was in my bag of Valtrex samples, and I found the number for the HIV testing clinic. I was nervous when I dialed. I knew I had to take an HIV test, but in a way, I didn't want to know. It was too stressful. The thought that I could die from having sex was frightening. The phone rang. I thought about hanging up. Maybe not knowing would be better. How would I go through the rest of my life if the test came back positive? Would I even live long enough to watch my son graduate from high school? How did I get myself into this mess? Oh, yeah, I was stupid.

A woman finally answered the phone, and I made an appointment for that Thursday. I would have the test in two days. I had the option of paying only five bucks and waiting two weeks for the results or paying $35 and getting them in a couple of days. I opted to pay more.

I didn't bother to ask the woman for directions. I figured I'd use the address that she had given me and look it up on MapQuest. I will never do that again. Always ask for directions because, believe it or not, people and clinics move. On that Thursday afternoon, I pulled up to a nasty, yellow, vacant building. I used my cell phone and got the correct directions. As I pulled away from the yellow building, I made a promise to myself. I vowed never to have unsafe sex again. I vowed never to be in this situation again. I promised myself to respect my body as much as I respect my computer. I never download anything because I am terrified of viruses.

Amazingly enough, I still arrived at the clinic on time. Being the Type-A person I am, I was way ahead of schedule anyway, in case I hit traffic or got lost. I checked in with the very nice lady at the reception desk, who had also given me directions when I called, all frazzled from in front of the icky yellow building. She told me to have a seat in the waiting room and that someone would call me.

I walked into the waiting room, and suddenly, I saw imaginary biohazard stickers on all the chairs. This was a VD clinic. What if I caught something worse just by sitting on one of the chairs? Luckily, I came to my senses and sat on the edge of the seat closest to the reception desk. I would have looked funny standing around when there were at least a dozen empty seats. I sat on the edge, partly to avoid leaning against the back of the chair and partly because it still hurt to sit.

A good-looking middle-aged man called my name. He smiled and said to follow him. Great. I was embarrassed already that I had to talk to a man about this. I usually choose female doctors. Because I was abused by men as a child, I didn't feel comfortable with being in a room alone with a male medical professional.

I had no choice here. I followed him into a room and sat in a chair across from him. He asked me why I was having an HIV test, and I told him. I said, "I was dating someone who gave me herpes, and I want to make sure he didn't give me anything else." I said it out loud. It felt wrong. It felt like a nightmare. I wanted to wake up.

Mr. Smiles talked to me for a few minutes. He asked me a bunch of questions that I could say no to, like: Have you had sex with a woman? (no.) Have you had sex with a man who has had sex with another man? (not to my knowledge) Have you ever had sex for drugs or money? (I laughed at this one.)

The questions were embarrassing, but they made me feel better. At least I could answer no to a lot of them. I didn't feel as sleazy as I had when I walked in. I was feeling better. Then, the counselor asked me when my first "exposure" to The Toad was. Exposure — now that's the truth. It wasn't a relationship; it was an extended exposure. I told him on July 17th, which was approximately three and a half months before. The counselor told me it can sometimes take up to four months for HIV antibodies to show. He asked me if I thought The Toad had been faithful. I told him I believed he had been because he was ALWAYS with me. The counselor recommended I test again in six months. My stomach sank.

The nice counselor brought me back to the lab, where a man with a thick German accent drew my blood. At first, I was nervous; I felt like I was surrounded by men, and I hated needles. I had had some terrible blood drawing experiences in the past, complete with bruising and needle twisting. But the odd thing is that I felt nothing. This man was a pro. I felt absolutely nothing, not even a pinch.

Waiting for my results was tortuous. It would take until Tuesday to get them. Tuesday was also the day that I had to do a big comedy show at the local performing arts hall. I called Fred, the promoter, and told him that if my HIV results were positive, I would not make it to the show. He told me I would be fine, and I asked him for six numbers for the lottery since he was psychic and all.

Results day finally arrived, and I drove to the clinic. At that time, they could not give a person HIV results over the phone. They (whoever makes these rules up) believed that patients needed counseling no matter what the results were. I was a nervous wreck. I cried in the car. I thought of my son growing up without his mommy. I was killing myself with grief.

I sat in the waiting room for what seemed like an eternity until the nice counselor called my name. I sat in the chair and looked at him like a trapped animal. He must have seen the fear in my eyes because he smiled even larger and said, "You're fine." I can't even describe the relief that went through me. I would not die, not this time. The counselor recommended that I still get tested again in six months and then sent me on my way.

2005 | Dating a REAL Prince

For two months, I plotted my future as a spinster. I relished the thoughts of chopping my long auburn hair into a crew cut and having a hysterectomy. I thought about how many cats I would adopt and how many Lifetime movies I could watch with those cats. I stocked up on Easy Mac and Ben and Jerry's "Chubby Hubby" so that I could put on as many pounds as I wanted. Freedom! I kept telling myself. That's really what I wanted — to be free of the whole dating scene. I also wanted to be free of ever having to tell someone that I had herpes. So, single I would stay. Yeah, right! This is me, after all.

A couple of weeks before I had begun dating The Toad, I forced myself (my mom forced me) to go to speed dating. Basically, a group of singles meet at a bar, each paying $40 for the privilege of doing so. The men sit at tables, and the women change seats every five minutes. Most of the seats are those high barstool-type chairs. I, being five foot even, on a big hair day, felt like I needed a step stool, or that step aerobics step I keep under my bed. Yes, it is as degrading as it sounds.

The first man that I "dated" was my son's dentist. He didn't recognize me, of course. He must have other patients or something. I'll admit that when I first sat down with him, I had dollar signs in my eyes. All I could think was "free fillings." Jewelry and fancy vacations did not even cross my mind. As a single mom, I was just focused on NOT having to pay for my son's dental work. Then the man spoke. This was the most strained conversation that I have ever had in my life. I instantly knew why the man was single. He had no game. I was so happy to hear the move-to-the-next-victim bell ring.

Anyway, most of the guys were BORING or complete jerks. One guy even watched football OVER MY HEAD while I tried to make the usual "What do you do? Where are you from?" small talk. I felt unattractive, and like I had wasted my time until I got to Chris's table.

Chris and his co-worker, George, were at about the fourth table that I visited. I instantly felt comfortable sitting next to Chris. It was like I could breathe again. His smile was warm, and he had (still does) a genuine sense of humor. I still remember our first conversation:

Him: What do you do?
Me: I'm a teacher and a stand-up comedian.
Him: At the same time?
Me: Usually, yes.

We both laughed. In the remaining 4 ½ minutes, we determined that we had a mutual acquaintance. Sheri worked for the same company as Chris, and her son was in my class at the Montessori school — small world. Though I felt comfortable with Chris, I felt like he was not happy with the fact that I had a child. He has since told me that this was not the case, but, for whatever reason, I thought he wasn't interested in me and was just being nice.

The bell rang, and I was off to sit with "Football over the head" guy, and Chris was presented with Floozy number five. Chris and I didn't exchange phone numbers because we both ASSUMED that "they" would match us up if there was an interest. WE WERE WRONG.

After I suffered through two more speed dates, I was told by the queen of all speed dating that I was on a 10-minute bathroom break. I found the facilities and took her advice. Like most bar bathrooms, this one was gross. So, I left. I was hungry and tired of telling people what I did for a living and where I was from. I just wanted to go home. I did, stopping to pick up a double cheeseburger at McDonalds on the way. I now call it my "Cinderella escape." Instead of leaving a shoe, I left a clue. I swear I did not mean for that to rhyme.

A couple of days later, I was home alone. Since it was summer, my son had gone to stay with his father for a while. I was working part-time and kind of bored, so, I did what all desperate people do — I placed an ad on that damn dating site and ended up with a toad. I dated The Toad for a while and you all know how that ended up. I was still dating The Toad when orientation day at school rolled around. I was meeting with new students and their parents when Sheri pulled me aside and said, "Chris wants to see you again."

After dating for a month, I was already not too impressed with The Toad, but I told Sheri, "I'm kind of seeing someone."

"Maybe you could date them both," she said.

"I can't do that," I told her. It's not that I have morals or values or anything (sarcasm); I'm just not coordinated enough to date two men at once. I already knew from what I did in my first marriage that cheating meant many lies to keep straight and a lot of extra shaving and showering — too much stress. Sheri went back to Chris with the bad news — Ms. Petty was dating someone.

About two months after that, I dumped The Toad on the day before Halloween. Three days after that, I found out that I had herpes. As you can imagine, I didn't exactly call Sheri and say, "Give Chris my number because I've got crotch sores for him." I wanted to crawl into a cave, a well-air-conditioned cave with cable, and hide from men.

Sheri didn't give up, though. She knew that Chris and I belonged together. She approached me at the school's Christmas party later that year and asked if I was still dating The Toad. When I said no, she got a big smile on her face and asked if she could give Chris my phone number.

"UGH! I hate talking on the phone. You can give him my email address." And she did. I didn't expect to hear from Chris. He was such a handsome and nice guy. I figured someone had already snatched him up.

Chris didn't email me until January. After a few witty messages, I gave him my phone number. The first time we talked on the phone, he apologized for waiting three weeks to get in touch with me. He said he figured I would be busy with family over the holidays. I informed him that my family consisted of me, my son, and my mom. We didn't really do much. Chris and I agreed to meet for lunch the following Monday.

It was Martin Luther King Jr. Day, a day off for me since I was a teacher. I ordered wine as soon as I sat down because I was nervous. Chris was jealous because he had to go back to work and could not have wine. All noon-time wine buzz jealousy aside, we really hit it off. Since this was our first time eating together, I tried to be dainty, and I ordered the crab cake appetizer for lunch. One small crab cake was placed in front of me shortly after that. Chris and I joked about how it did say crab CAKE not CAKES. I drove through McDonald's on the way home.

Our next date was at my house, where I was supervising a sleepover for my son and one friend. Chris dared to bring pizza and soda to a home filled with seven-year-old boy squeals. He brought pepperoni for them and a supreme pizza for the grown-ups. Since it was only our second date, I opted not to express my hatred for onions, mushrooms, and olives. I somehow choked down a piece of pizza with those vile toppings.

Our third date was our first adult date. Chris took me to a fancy restaurant where his friend was a waiter. I instantly showed my poor upbringing by being way too impressed with the crumb scraper. They didn't have those at McDonald's. Then, after looking over the menu for a long time, I ordered seared tuna, thinking it would be cooked all the way through, like a steak.

Nope. They put a raw slab of fish in front of me. "Um, I thought this would be cooked," I said while backing away from the plate. Chris and our waiter patiently explained that seared tuna was briefly seared (as the name suggests) on either side and left raw in the middle. I asked the waiter if the chef could cook it for me. Oddly enough, he agreed. I bet Chris left a big tip.

A couple of weeks after that, I was home sick with my son. Chris called to ask if I needed anything and I was out of Sprite, the only thing the boy would drink when he was sick. My new prince of a boyfriend stopped by on his way home from work with a bottle of Sprite. When Chris arrived with the Sprite, I made Richie come out of his room to say hello. As luck would have it, my son barfed on the dining room carpet shortly after greeting Chris. I quickly escorted him to the bathroom to clean him up and help him change his shirt. By the time I got back to the dining room, the puke was gone. Chris was on his knees, blotting the carpet with paper towels and holding a spray bottle of carpet cleaner in his hand. That's when I decided he could be in charge of all things icky.

A few months later, in July, Chris once again proved his talent for dealing with gross things. We were at Bonnaroo, which is a very crowded music festival that takes place on a farm in Themiddleofnowhere, Tennessee. It is not the place for a neurotic, claustrophobic, neat freak, but I went anyway. Shortly after we got there, I discovered that Port-O-Potties were my only bathroom option for the next three days. I wasn't counting on that. I stepped into the first available stall, armed with a small pack of Lysol wipes, and I immediately stepped out while gagging and dry heaving. "I can't do this," I told Chris. So, he did what any absolute prince of a man would do. He took the wipes and went into the stall. He came out about two minutes later and pronounced it ready for me. I went back in. He had cleaned the seat and threw an enormous amount of toilet paper into the potty itself, thus covering all evidence. This is when I knew I should marry him. Shortly after that, we got engaged.

2005: Here Comes the Groom

A couple of weeks after we got back from Bonnaroo, Chris walked in from the garage through the laundry room. By this time, we had purchased my little rental home from the landlord, and we were living together. As his dad said, we "put the cart before the horse." I wasn't thinking about horses or carts; my thoughts were on making dinner. I was putting the finishing touches on a lasagna before I put it in the oven.

Chris put a PetSmart bag on the island counter. "I got dog bones for Mario and Lola," he said. Mario, a black lab pit bull mix, was Chris's dog before we met. Now, along with our Maltese Lola, he was a part of our family. "They're cool. You should look at them," Chris told me.

I put the lasagna in the oven and walked to the island. I opened the bag and saw one large dog bone, one tiny dog bone, and one small jewelry box from Dunkin's Diamonds. "You ASS!" I said while pulling the box from the PetSmart bag.

Chris laughed and grabbed the ring from me. He got down on one knee in the kitchen and proposed. After he put the ring on my finger, we both hugged, laughed, and kissed at the same time.

We started talking about a wedding after dinner. I wanted to elope since this would be my second marriage. I didn't see the need for an actual wedding because there was no guarantee that a relationship would work. Chris had never been married. He told me that he watched his siblings get married and divorced, so he opted to wait for the right person. Chris said this would be his first and only wedding, so he wanted a real wedding with all of his family and friends. I agreed to be a bride again. After thinking about Florida weather, and the time needed to plan a wedding, we opted to set our date in mid-October.

We got married in a Unitarian church in Fort Myers on a beautiful Saturday in October. Chris was raised Catholic, I was raised without religion, and I did not want to convert, so the Unitarian church was a good comprise. The ceremony had some religious aspects, but it was also open to all religions.

The next day, we flew to Honolulu for our honeymoon. It was one of the few states that Chris had not yet visited, and of course, growing up on food stamps and being a single mom, I had not been to Hawaii. Aside from the long flight, during which Chris was not allowed to have a cigarette (his only vice), it was the perfect honeymoon location for us.

On the way there, I was thinking of all of the things that ruined my first marriage, aside from the fact that it never should have happened. I knew that I would never cheat on anyone again, and I haven't. I also knew that I needed to tone down my Type-A personality and not try to control everything. When we were getting dressed to go tour Pearl Harbor, and Chris put on an "I am a hero" T-shirt that he had received from donating to the United Way, I said nothing. I figured that he was a grown man, and he knew where we were going.

The tour went well, even with Chris having a nicotine fit while we were on the deck of the USS Missouri. After we had lunch on the ship and Chris had a much-needed cigarette, we walked around Pearl Harbor. We were headed to the bookstore when we met a really old World War II veteran who was a survivor of the attack. My stomach sank. I remembered what shirt Chris was wearing.

The veteran noticed Chris's shirt and asked, "You're a hero? What did you do?"

Being the supportive wife that I am, I looked at Chris and said, "I'll be looking at books." Then, I walked into the store, leaving him to tell the veteran that he had donated to the United Way. We both learned a lesson that day. I learned that if I see him wearing something inappropriate, it's okay for me to tell him. He learned to think about what he wears.

2005 | Parents, Palm Sunday, and a Period

It was the weekend before Easter in 2005. Chris and I had been dating for a couple of months and had already talked about getting married. We were in the beginning stages of buying the house I had been renting. We were moving fast and were very happy.

Now it was time for me to meet his super Catholic parents. By super Catholic, I don't mean they wore capes. I mean that they were very, very, very involved in their church. As Chris says, "They're Father Dick and Sister Dorothy who accidentally got married and had five kids."

And I was a divorced single mom, shacking up with their youngest son. I knew they were going to think I was total trash. I was a wee bit nervous spending the weekend at their house, in a separate bedroom from my love because, of course, we were not married yet.

Since it was a weekend, and the weekend before Easter, which I later learned involved Palm Sunday, we went to church. Allow me to pause and offer some TMI here. I was 33 and two years into crime-scene-level perimenopausal periods that were at their worst on day three of my cycle. Guess what day Palm Sunday fell on?

Though I was raised mostly without religion and tended to believe more in the Universal Kittens than Jesus, Mary, and stepdaddy Joseph, I had actually been to Catholic church a time or two. I knew there would be crackers I couldn't eat and some aerobic activity: stand, sit, kneel. I had never been to Catholic church on Palm Sunday. If you are unaware of what this means, let me explain. Palm Sunday is the longest service of the year, to my knowledge. It lasts at least three days. I'm only exaggerating slightly. The aerobic exercises are taken up a notch, and the standing lasts FOREVER.

My friends who have periods know where this is going. Soon, the rest of you will, too, but I must pause and explain that Chris's parents preferred to eat breakfast after church. So, I had not eaten, which means I had not been able to take Motrin (that stuff eats my stomach but really helps with cramps). I was already hungry and crampy. Cue the standing.

Every time I stood, I felt my uterus trying to get rid of its entire lining in one minute. After a few rounds of sit, kneel, stand for five years, I started to feel weak, and I broke into a cold sweat. Nausea had decided to come out to play.

I carefully excused myself while everyone was standing and went to the bathroom. I stayed in there a long time and put cold water on the back of my neck. I changed diapers and tried to pull myself together. When I exited the bathroom, Chris was standing there.

"Please tell your parents I have my period!" I said to him, while hugging him. "I don't want them to think I'm pregnant."

He laughed.

"Seriously! They will hate me!" Chris hugged me and assured me they would not hate me but he would tell them.

Somehow, I went back into church and got through the rest of the service. We went to breakfast afterwards, and I was able to chug down some Motrin with my coffee and French Toast. Chris had managed to share my TMI with them when I wasn't around. They knew what was up with me.

When we got back to the house, Chris ran for the hall bathroom. He probably had too much coffee and bacon. While he was sitting in the bathroom, which did NOT HAVE A FART FAN, his mom decided to show me all of her stained glass work in the hallway right outside of the bathroom door.

We stopped in front of a framed stained glass crane about six feet from the bathroom door, and she grabbed my arm and looked at me with this really stern look. I thought, Oh shit. Here it comes. She's going to tell me to leave her son alone, that I'm not good enough for him. Nope.

"You make my son very happy," she said, looking right into my eyes.

"I try," I stammered.

"Welcome to the family," she said. My eyes watered a bit as I thanked her.

Then the toilet flushed. The water ran in the sink as Chris washed his hands before walking out of the bathroom and pretending he had not heard every word.

We enjoyed the rest of the day sitting on the patio with his parents, sharing stories, and getting to know each other. Six months later, Chris and I were married, and I was not pregnant then either.

After Chris's mom, Dorothy, died in 2013, his father gave me the stained glass crane. I still have it. I think about that first visit whenever I look at it and, of course, on every Palm Sunday.

2006 | Love and Vomit

I wiped barf from my chin with the washcloth Chris had handed me. "I'm sorry!" I said to my new husband, from my seat on the floor in the doorway to our bathroom. I had chocolate martini vomit on my shirt, my chin, and the floor.

He laughed and replied, "This is nothing! I was in a fraternity. And I did tell you to go ahead." He took the used rag from me, wiped the floor, and got up to throw it in the laundry room.

That's right. It was his fault, and not just because he made the chocolate martinis. Chris had told me to puke. He wasn't specific enough. He should have directed me to crawl the three feet to the toilet before letting go.

This was our first New Year's Eve together, and it had started out without sickness. We had been married for two and a half months by this point. We were planning a quiet evening at home with another couple we were friends with. This ended up lasting until about eleven when I stumbled out of the living room and into our bedroom, where Chris found me sitting on the floor.

He came back from the laundry room and kneeled next to me. "I guess we should have eaten more than salad, huh." He chuckled. He was pretty drunk, too, but not on the floor drunk like I was. We had just started the South Beach Diet that evening and had eaten some sort of low-carb salad for dinner, and that's it. No crackers or hors d'oeuvres or any traditional New Year's Eve snacks. Just lettuce, chicken breast, and chocolate martinis. I had two and a half martinis (our glasses were huge) before my body informed me they were coming back up.

Earlier that evening, we had been sitting in our small Cape Coral living room, chatting, drinking, and watching some New Year's Eve show with our friends. This couple was smart and brought beer to drink, which they stuck to after trying a chocolate martini. To me, beer is like bread soda. I've never really liked it, and honestly, it doesn't work fast enough. I've been a big vodka fan since my early 20s, actually since age 20. In South Florida, male servers never carded young women at bars, so I ordered vodka cranberries to my heart's content.

Chris went back out to the living room, leaving me to brush my teeth and change clothes. He told our guests they were welcome to stay but, "Lisa's sick and going to bed." Well, this will come as a surprise, but they opted to leave. I don't blame them. Chris was probably slurring by this time himself. He did not vomit, but he told me he was finishing half-finished drinks in the kitchen while he was cleaning up. That's not good.

Once I got into bed, the room started spinning. I tried to put one foot on the floor to stabilize the room (because that works), but at oompa loompa height, it's tough to lie on a bed and put your foot on the floor. I eventually passed out, and I guess my husband did the same.

The next morning, I was so happy that our eight-year-old son was with my ex-husband. I didn't want him to see us like this. We were a wreck. Chris and I laid on the couch all day, drinking water and Gatorade and reading. It took the whole day to recover.

2006 | The Snappiest Place on Earth

"FUCK YOU!" That is what my mom said to me while we were standing in line behind a blond family with matching Mickey ears. That was her response to me quietly calling her on her bullshit. What bullshit, you ask? Giving me parenting advice.

Our eight-year-old son was getting antsy in the long line for Soarin at EPCOT, so he was jumping and hanging from Chris's neck. I didn't want to have to leave the line to go deal with a broken neck at the ER, so I said, "STOP!" and pulled him away from Chris.

My mother, being ever so protective of my son, said, "Lisa, he's just a child!"

A hundred scenes of her hitting me and screaming at me went through my head in seconds. I looked at her, and through gritted teeth, I said, "I know, mother."

Janet wasn't as clueless about her parenting style as she pretended to be, and I knew this even though I pretended not to. That's when the "fuck you" came into play.

Chris, who had quit smoking three days earlier, chomped extra hard on his Nicorette, looked at my mom like he might fly at her, and said, "NOBODY SPEAKS TO MY WIFE THAT WAY!"

Mom backed down and was quiet the rest of our time in line. We were able to enjoy Soarin' without any more profanities or injuries. After the ride, we walked over to the World Showcase portion of EPCOT. We went to the restaurant in "England" and had fish and chips. My mom probably felt less than loved by Chris and me, so she did what she often did to make up for things: she tried to pay for lunch. Chris and I did not allow this because we knew she was on her second bankruptcy, and there was no way any of her cards would work. Even if they did, we would end up moving money into her account, which I was on, to pay the credit card bill. She knew she had no money, but she tried to pay for an expensive theme park lunch.

I wish I could say it was a pleasant trip after that episode, but it wasn't. My mom was miserable all three days due to her own stubbornness. Instead of wearing sneakers and socks, she wore nurse shoes without socks. My mom's freshly-styled, naturally-curly hair got wet in Animal Kingdom on a ride. She was already sweaty because she refused to wear shorts, so her curls were already popping out. Once that big splash of water landed on Mom's head, she was so pissed off at everyone. Her hair was a shrine, and she fought those curls with once-a-week visits to the hairdresser for a blowout and a couple of coats of hair spray. Then, she tried to avoid rain and sweat — in south Florida.

For the rest of the trip, she complained about the weather, about her hair, about anything and everything. At one point, when we were in a shop on the way out, I looked at her and said, "Why are you like this?" I felt brave enough to call her on her behavior since I knew she couldn't hit me anymore. She knew that, too, and she just looked at me like I was an idiot and turned away.

When Chris and I were finally alone in our hotel room, I promised him I would never invite my mom on a trip to Disney again. He said, "Feel free not to limit it to Disney." I didn't. We never took my mom on a trip again. I was choosing my prince over the wicked witch.

2007 | **Moving on Up North**

It was a beautiful January day in Cape Coral, Florida. The sky was blue, and the humidity was low, at least by Florida standards. Chris and I stood by the front window and watched the moving truck parallel park in front of our house.

"Well, I guess we are really doing this," Chris said while putting his arm around me. Richie was at school for his last day in Florida. Chris, who had moved to different states as a kid, said it was better if he didn't see all of our stuff get loaded on a truck.

After the truck was loaded and Richie was home, we would be off to begin a new life in Fort Wayne, Indiana. I was excited about the move. Chris and I had gone on a house shopping trip earlier that month and I fell in love with Fort Wayne's small-town charm. As someone who had been looking for Mayberry all her life, I thought I had found it. The schools were better rated, crime was lower, and the cost of living was super low.

Chris had accepted a job with Vera Bradley, the quilted purse company. Being a Kate Spade girl before I even knew what Kate Spade was, I wasn't thrilled about the multi-colored busy purses, but I was eager to escape South Florida. By this time, I was working full-time for an online University. My job traveled with me.

When we first moved into our house in Fort Wayne, Richie and I were mesmerized by the snow. He put on a coat, hat, and gloves and went out to make snowballs on our first day there. I put on boots every time I went outside, even if it was just to get the mail. I was a newbie. I thought the snow was pretty, but I was also afraid to slip and fall. I was also afraid to drive in it. I kept my Florida plate on my car until Spring just to warn the natives that I was dangerous.

Richie started his second half of fourth grade the day after we moved in and he made friends quickly. The school system there was a little ahead of the one in Florida. They had already learned cursive and Florida had not begun teaching it yet. To this day, Richie cannot read or write cursive.

Chris and I made friends, too. After a good homesickness and crying spell, Chris encouraged me to join the Newcomers Club because it had helped his mom so much when they moved. I looked them up and went to my first book club meeting at a beautiful house near me. Coming from Florida, I thought my two-story Indiana home was fancy, but this house was amazing.

After five years in Fort Wayne, I felt like I would live there forever. It wasn't the Mayberry I thought it would be, and teen Richie made some sketchy friends in high school, but I wasn't planning on leaving. I was comfortable.

Then, Chris told me he had found a new job in Columbus, Ohio. I knew he had been interviewing, and we had talked about getting out of a one-horse town. Other than Vera Bradley, there wasn't a company where Chris could continue his career in corporate retail. Columbus, Ohio had lots of choices, and we already knew people there. While I was sad to say goodbye to my Fort Wayne friends, I was looking forward to getting Richie away from some of his friends, especially his girlfriend.

We moved in the summer, which is not the right thing to do if you are moving a teen to another state. Richie did not have any local friends so he spent a lot of time on Skype with the girlfriend. She made us all miserable for months without even being in the same state. When school started, and Richie met new people, his girlfriend would express her jealousy from afar.

While we lived in the Midwest, I flew to South Florida at least twice a year to visit my mom and attend conferences for the online university I worked for. The conferences were in Fort Lauderdale, and my mother lived in an apartment building in Pembroke Pines. The apartment was much tinier than the Atrium Apartment she had lived in for twenty years. After John died, the landlord doubled the rent since John wasn't there to do maintenance tasks for him anymore. Mom could not afford the rent, so she moved into a subsidized building about twenty minutes away.

During one of my trips home, my flight back to Indiana was canceled. I had to go to baggage claim, get my luggage, and find a cab to a hotel that Chris was able to book for me. I really didn't want to go back to my mom's apartment, where I had been sleeping on the couch. I felt guilty about not wanting to spend that extra time with her, but Chris reminded me that he thought it was amazing that I even still talked to her after the upbringing I had. I couldn't imagine cutting off all contact with my mother. I was all she had. Tony had moved and never gave us his new phone number or address when I was 19, shortly after I met his son.

I walked towards the baggage carousel, feeling sad and impatient. I wanted to go home to Chris and Richie. Then, I noticed the woman standing six feet from me. Her dark hair looked familiar. Then I heard her voice.

"Hillary!" I said. I hadn't seen Hillary in at least 12 years by this point.

"Oh my god! Lisa!" she gave me a hug and introduced her husband. They had just returned from Boston.

Hillary and I caught up while we waited for our bags. I told her about the canceled flight and being disappointed but relieved the pilot did not try to fly through the dense fog over Indiana. We chatted away for a few minutes, and it felt like we were back at Olsen Middle again, BFFs. Before Hillary left to go home with her husband, she leaned in close and told me, "I'm pregnant, only eight weeks, so we aren't telling anyone yet." I hugged her and congratulated her. I was so happy that she trusted me enough to tell me even though we had not been close since middle school.

Our time in the Midwest came to a close in 2019. The company Chris was working for laid off a lot of people, and he was one of them. He tried to find a job in Ohio, but there were no open positions for him. He ended up finding a job in Winston-Salem, North Carolina. We were moving back down south, but not all the way to Florida. We lasted eighteen months before we moved to our forever state, Arizona.

2017 | Those Fucking Clowns

In September of 2017, we went on a family trip to Florida to visit my mom and Chris's dad. This also allowed Richie an extra visit with his dad. Richie spent summers, Christmas break, and Spring break with his dad and step-mom when we lived in the Midwest. Richie ended up moving to Orlando in 2019 to complete his Bachelor's Degree, so he didn't move to North Carolina with us. At the time of this visit, we were all still living in Ohio.

My husband, son, and I were sitting in my mother's tiny, humid living room in her subsidized apartment in Pembroke Pines on the Saturday of Labor Day weekend. Things were going okay. She was chatting away, as usual. My mom loved to talk.

We were sitting on the couch across from her cream-colored wall unit, where the TV and her knick-knack collection lived. Mom started pointing to knick-knacks and talking about where they came from. Then, she pointed up at three sad-looking, chipped, ceramic clowns and said, "Lisa, didn't Rod give those to you?" My stomach instantly cramped. Why would she bring that up? Rod was anything but a positive memory for both of us.

I wanted to say, "Yes, mother. Yes. That man who beat you and molested me for seven years. That Rod. Yes, he gave me those cheap-ass stupid clowns that you insist on keeping and shoving in my face like they don't make me want to vomit on the cheap, low-pile carpet. It's like you had a lobotomy and forgot reality. Yes. He gave those to me." Instead, I said, "Uh huh," and excused myself to go to the bathroom, taking my purse with me. While I was in there,

I took two Ativan and some deep breaths. I was close to having a panic attack just from hearing Rod's name. I hadn't thought about him in years, and in a matter of seconds, my mom brought him right back into my brain.

I think Rod knew he sucked as a boyfriend and a person. He knew, on some level, that beating women and molesting little girls was wrong. I think that is why he was always trying to buy my mom's and my forgiveness. Rod was always buying my mom flowers or some other "I'm sorry" present after a big fight. He bought me stuff, too, like these stupid fucking clowns.

My mom always loved knick-knacks. I have never understood this, as they do nothing but collect dust. Anyway, Rod used to buy her little ceramic things. I guess he figured I would love them, too, so he bought me three little clowns. For most of my childhood, they were on a shelf in my bathroom, above the toilet. When I moved out, I left them there because I had no reason to want to keep anything Rod gave me. I guess my mom thought they were keepable.

That was the last time I saw my mom in person. In 2019, I received the call I knew would come someday, given her refusal to move in with us or accept visiting help. Believe me; we tried to get her out of that apartment and closer to us. She said no.

My phone rang when I was getting out deli meat from the refrigerator in my Ohio kitchen to make a sandwich. I had just gotten home from a doctor's visit that included fasting bloodwork, and I was starving. I closed the refrigerator and picked up my phone. I looked down at the screen and saw that my ex-husband, Richard, was calling. I thought to myself, "This is either really good news or really bad news." Richard and I didn't talk on the phone often now that Richie was an adult.

I heard him crying as soon as I answered the phone. I knew what was coming. "Lisa, I'm sorry, but your mom. They found her dead in her apartment." Since Richard lived close to my mom, he was the emergency number they had on file. The police called him after finding her while doing a wellness check. The mailman noticed she wasn't getting her mail, so the building manager, "One-eyed Bastard" as my mom referred to him, called the police. The police called Richard and then me, after Richard gave him my number.

From what they saw, my mom had been dead for a few days. She had been sick to her stomach in the bathroom and fell. There was blood and other fluids from the bathroom to the living room recliner, where they found her. Hearing this was really hard, and my feelings were complicated. I felt guilty for not being able to persuade her to move closer to us. I felt sad because I knew Richie would be very upset. He was close to his grandma, and she was a much better grandmother than mother. I also felt relief. I was 47, and I finally didn't have to worry about my mother. While I was sad, I was free.

Richard handled letting in the hazmat crew to clean the apartment. He took pictures and sent them to Chris. Chris asked me if I wanted to see them, and I said, "No." The pictures in my head were bad enough. After hearing about how his grandmother died and spending some time alone crying (he requested space), Richie made Chris and I promise that we would live with him when we were old.

Chris, Richie, Richie's girlfriend, and I flew down to Pembroke Pines to clear out Mom's apartment. The first thing that Chris did when we got in was grab those three clowns and throw them in the trash, making sure they broke as they hit the bottom of the bag which was against the floor.

2024 | My Man and the Sea

"Come out here and take an ocean selfie with me," Chris said from the balcony of our room on the Discovery Princess. I got up from the couch, where I had been attempting to grade essays on less than stellar internet during our long sea day. The ocean has always made me nervous as it had been forced on me during my entire life in Florida.

I stepped out on the balcony, gripped the railing, and looked up into Chris's green eyes, making sure the whites were not yellow. He looked so happy, so I tried not to ruin it by being obvious with my quick color check. I snuggled into Chris and let him take the "ussie" with the ocean in the background. Then, I hugged him extra hard and went back to grading.

We had gotten some uncertain health news right before the cruise to Alaska, which we had always referred to as a bucket list item for Chris, and now, using that term makes the pit of my stomach pinch me. Chris had things growing in his pancreas. The cysts had been there for seven years, discovered accidentally after an MRI for chest pain. They hadn't really affected his life for a long time, but now two enzymes in his recent bloodwork were high, and he needed to have another MRI when he had just had one six months earlier. He would be having this MRI when we got back from the cruise. Chris's mother died from pancreatic cancer in 2013, so all of this was a bit disturbing, but we didn't want it to spoil this dream vacation.

The Monday after getting back to our home in Phoenix, where we moved after spending a year in North Carolina, we drove to the imaging center. I waited in the waiting room while Chris had his test. He had an appointment with his doctor on Wednesday to learn the results and next steps. We had already scared ourselves playing Google doctors on the internet. I told him I wanted to go with him to the appointment to be sure we asked all of the questions and took notes. On the morning of the appointment, I tested positive for COVID.

Chris didn't like my idea of "wearing a mask and pretending it's a cold." He's not a rebel like me. So, we did the next best thing: Chris called me from the exam room and put me on speaker. I was exhausted and very congested by the virus, but I still managed to stay awake and listen as carefully as I was able. Overall, the news wasn't as bad as we had been expecting. No surgery was needed at this time. Chris would need to repeat bloodwork in six months and then have another MRI in a year.

In his relief of hearing this news, Chris forgot to mention the epigastric pain he'd been having. When the doctor asked him if he had any more concerns, Chris said, "No." Lucky for him, his Type-A-even-when-sick wife was on the phone. "What about the upper left side pain you've been having?" I said loudly, due to my hearing aids not working well with my congested ears.

Once the doctor heard this, it was decided that Chris would have an upper endoscopy again. He had one in Ohio when they first found the cysts seven years earlier. I was relieved the doctor was being thorough. I had never met Chris's current gastroenterologist in person, but his voice was strong, and he recommended having the endoscopy as soon as possible.

When Chris was recovering from his upper endoscopy, I finally met his gastroenterologist. The doctor shook my hand firmly and looked into my eyes as he told me the results. Since I'm hard of hearing, I misheard him at first.

"All good?" I asked after he spoke.

"No. Not good," he said, looking at me with serious brown eyes.

"I'm sorry. I don't hear well," I told him while leaning forward over Chris, while rubbing my husband's arm. I always end up apologizing for my hearing as though I had chosen not to hear.

The doctor waved off my apology and continued. "The hiatal hernia is worse. There is a lot of acid damage, all the way down to the small intestine," the doctor said.

Well, shit. That is not what I expected. Usually, when Chris or I have one of these scopes we get the all-clear. I said, "Oh," not knowing what else to say, and waited for the doctor to finish.

"I took some biopsies. We should have the results in a week or two. I sent in a new prescription. He needs to start it in the morning. He can take the Pepcid tonight, but then he has to stop."

I nodded, shook the doctor's hand again before he left the recovery area, and sat down in the chair next to Chris, who was still asleep. I patted his arm and tried to wake him while the nurse came in to check on him. I was worried and I probably would have cried if I weren't on Prozac.

Now, here we are, trying to eat healthier foods, avoiding alcohol, and going to the gym more often hoping Chris doesn't require a Whipple Procedure to remove the huge chunk of his pancreas that has cysts. We are also still waiting for biopsy results from the endoscopy.

Of course, I'm going through all the worst-case scenarios. It took me 33 years to find my prince. I met a few frogs and a toad along the way. I had to learn how to have a great relationship by observing and having shitty ones. I wouldn't be a card carrying anxiety patient if I didn't worry about losing him. Questions roll through my brain. What if he has stomach cancer? What if he has to have half of his pancreas removed? What if he has to be on insulin the rest of his life? All of these questions go through my head every time I look at him. And when I get frustrated with him for not doing whatever mundane household task he said he would do, I remember all of this and I remember what is really important – waking up every day with Chris.

Halloween, 1976

The only picture of me with my dad, 1976.

Photo Gallery 185

Miss Kitty and me, 1979.

Mom, Tony and me, 1979.

Marilyn and me modeling in Burdine's, 1984.

Hillary and me, summer 1985.

Mom and John getting married in Las Vegas, fall 1985.

John and me, 1985.

Me discovering alcohol, 1986.

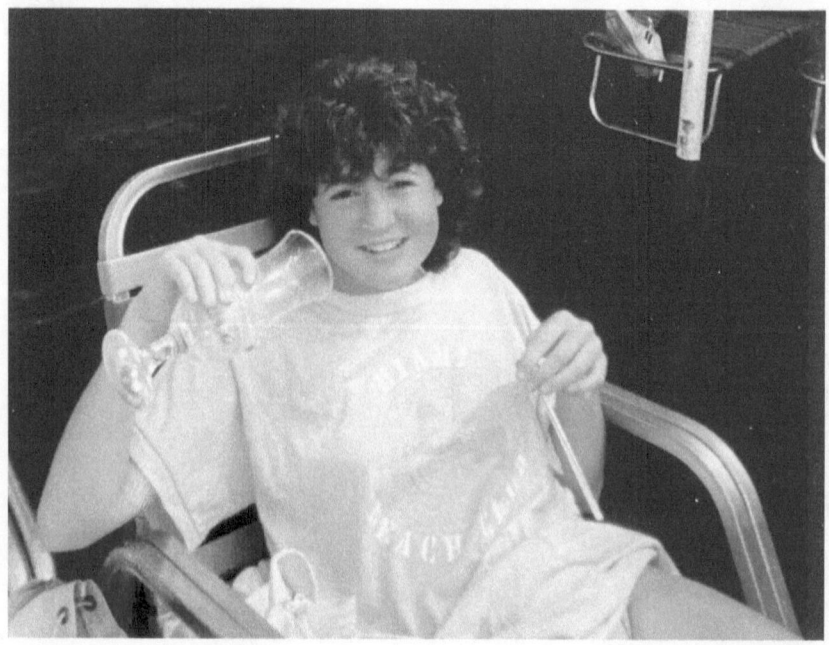
Theresa also discovered alcohol, 1986.

Richie walking me down the aisle, 2005.

Nicole, Fran and Mom at my wedding, 2005.

Chris, Richie and me, summer 2005.

Chris and me on our Alaskan cruise, 2024.

Virtual Hugs

A big hug to all of you who took the plunge and read this book. I'm so lucky to have readers like you.

Thank you, Chris for laughing at dark humor, tolerating my stoicism, allowing me to discuss our homelife online, and for loving me, the boy, and all of the furry creatures we have had in our two decades together.

Richie, thank you for showing me how to be myself and embrace my creativity and oddness. You are the perfect son for me. The next book will be all about us. I'm proud of you.

Liz, thank you for sticking with this crazy family. You've been through a lot with us and I am ever grateful for your kindness.

I am very grateful for my beta readers: Laura Richardson, Brook Phillips, Holly Wright, Lynn Van Antwerp, Stacey Roberts, Robert Kovacs, and Ruth DeWit. I appreciated your honest feedback and I hope you won't be afraid to read the final version of the book. I promise it is better than what you read months ago.

I'd like to thank my close friends and chosen family.

Fran Singleton, Nicole Greenberg, Bobby Singleton, John Mei, you helped to create my "normal" family.

Hillary Reynolds, Theresa Eckert, Marilyn Campanella, you helped me to be a better person by example and you made me feel like I fit in with the cool kids. Hillary, you also taught me how to dress like a normal teen girl.

Jaye and Laura Richardson, Thank you for being our travel companions, pickleball partners, and fellow steakhouse aficionados.

Danny Martinez, you were the brother/BFF I always needed and finally found. Thank you for being a friend and an uncle to Richie.

Genna Freeborn, thank you for being my friend and local Bulldog.

Brook Phillips, thank you for being a comforting, understanding friend with a dark sense of humor.

My editor Christie Zgourides at CZ Editing. Thank you for helping me fine tune this memoir after ten years of drafting. I look forward to working with you on the next book.

Melanie McGaughey, the developmental editor who enlightened me to the fact that memoirs needed story arcs, too. I appreciate your taking the time to meet with me.

Thanks to my mother, Janet, for making me the strong, stoic, sarcastic person I am today.

• • •

Let's keep in touch! Follow me on lisagerardywriter.com, Facebook, and Instagram. My next memoir will focus on parenting after surviving a traumatic childhood and will be published in May 2026. Stay tuned!

www.ingramcontent.com/pod-product-compliance
Lightning Source LLC
LaVergne TN
LVHW091542070526
838199LV00002B/174